ADVANCE PRAISE

"With this groundbreaking research on bias in the workplace, Sylvia Hewlett, Ripa Rashid, and Laura Sherbin bring a fresh perspective. Their ability to quantify the cost to companies when employees feel the sting of bias—and to point toward ways companies can prevent that sting from happening—will help employers add important next steps beyond bias awareness training to truly improve the experience, performance, and productivity of employees."

—Ella Bell Smith, Founder and President, Ascent;
Professor of Business Administration,
Tuck School of Business, Dartmouth University

"*Disrupt Bias* offers a novel approach to the persistent problem of bias in the workplace, based on remarkably thorough study of where bias occurs, why perceptions are reality, and what companies must do to alter the inevitable bias that occurs without proactive leadership action."

—Amy C. Edmondson, Novartis Professor of Leadership and
Management, Harvard Business School;
Author, *Teaming: How Organizations Learn,
Innovate and Compete in the Knowledge Economy*

"This book is a blueprint for addressing bias and advancing an inclusive leadership culture by providing relevant and engaging examples that all readers can easily relate to."

—Rosalind L. Hudnell, President, Intel Foundation;
Vice President of Corporate Affairs, Intel Corporation

DISRUPT BIAS DRIVE VALUE

A New Path toward Diverse, Engaged, and Fulfilled Talent

DISRUPT BIAS
DRIVE VALUE

New Path toward Diverse, Engaged, and Fulfilled Talent

SYLVIA ANN HEWLETT
RIPA RASHID
LAURA SHERBIN

A CENTER FOR TALENT INNOVATION PUBLICATION • NEW YORK, NY

CENTER
FOR **TALENT**
INNOVATION

THIS IS A CENTER FOR TALENT INNOVATION PUBLICATION

A Vireo Book | Rare Bird Books
453 South Spring Street, Suite 302
Los Angeles, CA 90013
rarebirdbooks.com

FIRST TRADE PAPERBACK ORIGINAL EDITION

Set in Minion
Printed in the United States

10 9 8 7 6 5 4 3 2 1

Publisher's Cataloging-in-Publication data

Names: Hewlett, Sylvia Ann, 1946-, author. | Rashid, Ripa, author. | Sherbin,
Laura, author.
Title: Disrupt bias , drive value : a new path towards diverse , engaged , and
fulfilled talent / by Sylvia Ann Hewlett, Ripa Rashid, and Laura Sherbin.
Series: Center for Talent Innovation
Description: Includes bibliographical references and index. | First Trade
Paperback Original Edition | A Genuine Vireo Book | New York, NY; Los
Angeles, CA: Rare Bird Books, 2017.
Identifiers: ISBN 978-1-947856-07-3
Subjects: LCSH Diversity in the workplace. | Discrimination in employment. |
Minority professional employees—United States. | Personnel management—
United States. | Corporate culture—United States. | Multiculturalism—United
States. | BISAC BUSINESS & ECONOMICS / Human Resources & Personnel
Management
Classification: LCC HF5549.5.M5 .H49 2017 | DDC 658.3008—dc23

To the courageous change agents who have been at the heart of this research:

Rohini Anand
Redia Anderson
Ann Bohara
Cynthia Bowman
Yvonne Breitenfeld
Kathryn Burdett
Jennifer Correa
Janessa Cox
Ray Dempsey
Heide Gardner
Lisa Gutierrez
Wanda Hope
Erika Irish Brown
Devray Kirkland
Loren Monroe-Trice
Angela Morris
Donna Pedro
Alisa Rodway
Stephanie Roemer
Samantha Santos
Diana Solash
Maria Stolfi
Eileen Taylor
Karyn Twaronite
Jacqueline Welch

PROJECT TEAM

Bill Carroll, Research Intern

Isis Fabian, Senior Research Associate

Kennedy Ihezie, Vice President,
Strategic Outreach and Engagement

Pooja Jain-Link, Vice President,
Associate Director of Research

Melinda Marshall, Executive Vice President,
Senior Editor

Silvia Marte, Senior Communications Associate

Michael Rizzotti, Research Associate

Louisa Smith, Data Visualization and Illustration

Julia Taylor Kennedy, Executive Vice President,
Director of Publications

Tai Wingfield, Senior Vice President of
Communications

Emilia Yu, Research Associate

CONTENTS

INTRODUCTION

The Wrong Lesson Learned

It's perhaps the most famous case study in the young history of attempts to combat bias. In 1952, the Boston Symphony Orchestra introduced "blind auditions": to reduce gender bias in hiring, orchestra directors held auditions behind a screen.[1]

As the legend goes, the intervention appeared at first to have a surprising result: that there was no bias in the audition process. The screen made little difference in who made it past the first round of auditions. Then, suspecting that the click-clack of high heels permitted judges to identify women as they entered, the hiring committee asked the musicians to take off their shoes. Suddenly, the judges could focus on the music itself—and far more women made it through to the second round of auditions.

Other orchestras began adopting the Boston Symphony's approach in the 1970s. By the 1990s, many saw increases in the number of female players. The New York Philharmonic, for example, reached 35 percent female musicians by 1997—a dramatic increase over having zero female players for decades. One study of eleven major orchestras found that up to 55 percent of their increase in new female hires could be attributed to blind auditions.[2]

The broader impact of blind auditions has been revolutionary. Not only have they spread across the music world, they also serve as a parable for bias busting in business books.[3] A sure sign of a legend, parts of the story even appear to be apocryphal—we couldn't trace the high heels detail past secondary sources.

High heels or no, the tale of the Boston Symphony Orchestra's blind auditions—and peer-reviewed research about their impact—has helped many business leaders understand the enormous role bias plays in how they hire, evaluate, and promote employees. It has also kicked off an enormous body of scholarly work on bias.[4] Unfortunately, the insights many have drawn from this intervention neglect its most important lesson.

Rightly convinced that bias exists and that it must be largely unconscious—most business leaders must tell themselves that they're choosing the most qualified person for a given position—organizations have invested heavily in bias awareness training. The idea is to make us all aware of our biases so that we can recognize them and resist acting on them.

Yet there's little evidence that bias awareness training accomplishes its goals. There's even evidence, as we'll discuss below, that it may do more harm than good. And the focus on bias awareness ignores the Boston Symphony's most important lesson: that you must pinpoint where bias is happening, and then create *a system* (such as a screen and shoeless musicians) that mitigates that bias or prevents it from influencing decisions.

Taking the path that most bias-busting programs have missed, this book aims to offer a new, comprehensive lens on bias. Our approach begins not with cultivating awareness of bias among leaders, but with studying the experience of bias among those who are led. We map out where bias is most clearly felt, measure how it costs organizations, and offer targeted interventions designed to maximize business value—interventions that neither lay all the blame on individual managers, nor require them to constantly police themselves for biased unconscious impulses.

What we offer, instead, is a picture of where bias actually occurs in organizations. Based on a survey, online and in-person focus groups, interviews, and our expertise in the diversity and inclusion space, we've created a way to understand bias as employees feel it. We've identified key conditions that reduce the likelihood that an employee will feel bias. Finally, we give leaders a playbook, advising them how to create those conditions through systemic interventions. Hardly as simple as putting up a screen or changing the carpet, we believe these interventions will help mitigate individuals' experiences of bias at your company.

We'll begin this book as we began our research: with a look at why current anti-bias programs aren't achieving satisfactory results.

PART ONE
A NEW LENS ON BIAS

1

Diversity in Leadership is Business-Critical—and Elusive

There's no shortage of research making the link between diversity and the upside for businesses. For one thing, the talent pool in the US and many other countries is increasingly diverse, making the question of bias more and more important. According to US government statistics, the percentage of non-Latino[5] whites in the labor force will fall to under 50 percent by 2050.[6] It's crucial that this increasingly diverse pool enter a workplace that will allow the best talent to thrive. And with so many companies entering new markets in foreign countries—and in diverse communities within their home countries—building a bias-free workplace is also a competitive necessity for businesses seeking growth.

The importance of diversity is particularly significant at management levels, and research demonstrates strong links between diverse leadership and business outcomes. The Center for Talent Innovation (CTI)'s report *Innovation, Diversity, and Market Growth* found, among many other advantages, that employees in publicly traded companies with diverse leadership—defined as displaying at least three kinds of both inherent diversity (gender, race, age, religious background, socioeconomic background, sexual orientation, disability, nationality) and acquired diversity (cultural fluency, generational savvy, gender smarts, social media skills, cross-functional knowledge, global mindset, military experience, language skills)—are 45 percent more likely to report market share growth and 70 percent more likely to report capturing new markets.[7]

With the upside of diverse leadership clear, organizations' quests to mitigate bias in their ranks have escalated. Many are devoting significant resources to the effort, allocating more and more of these resources to bias awareness training.

THE CURRENT STANDARD: THE IMPLICIT ASSOCIATION TEST

Bias awareness training usually starts with the computer-based Implicit Association Test (IAT). The IAT began in 1995, when psychologists Anthony Greenwald and Mahzarin R. Banaji pioneered the theory of "implicit social cognition."[8] Based on this theory, they created the IAT as a way to measure bias.

The IAT asks test takers to quickly sort pairings of words and images into positive and negative categories. It instantly generates results that tell test takers whether they had more trouble associating positive characteristics with a given identity—in other words, whether they are biased against a certain social group. Millions of visitors have taken the IAT online through a program called Project Implicit.[9] Seventy-five percent of those who took the IAT for race showed a reflexive preference for whites.[10]

The IAT is designed to reveal unconscious biases we harbor based on social and behavioral preferences. Its results send a powerful message: we all hold biases we may not be aware of and risk making poor decisions as a result.

BIAS BUSTING IS BIG MONEY

Across the US, corporations have embraced awareness training based on the IAT as the pillar of bias-disruption and diversity strategies. Each year, hundreds of thousands of individuals take the IAT online,[11] and many managers go through training based on its theoretical framework. Many have also heard seminars or lectures about bias from Banaji herself.

The IAT is undeniably an appealing tool. For a start, there's the fast pace: it only takes about ten minutes. Then there's the usually eye-opening result: bias lurks inside most of us. The IAT manages to be quick and exciting while having a seemingly significant and immediate impact—not common characteristics of corporate training sessions. The IAT takes the complex theories that sociologists might use to describe bias's toll—for example, Mary P. Rowe's groundbreaking work on micro-inequities—and translates them for busy company executives without much patience for theory.[12] It's no surprise that the test is popular, and that work based on the IAT has become a profitable cottage industry.

As part of the $8 billion-a-year diversity training industry, workshops intended to raise awareness of unconscious bias generate substantial revenues.[13] Anti-bias training is particularly popular in Silicon Valley, where tech titans like Facebook and Google mandate it,[14] and a similar trend is on the rise among Fortune 500 corporations as a whole.[15] According to one global consultant specializing in unconscious bias training, 50 percent of large US employers with diversity programs are projected to provide such training by 2019.[16]

The IAT has many virtues. It provides a clear explanatory framework for interpreting corporate realities: that we all make rapid decisions informed by biases we hold in our unconscious minds. The IAT provides awareness of the specific biases we hold, so that (in theory) we can work to resist them when making decisions.

For many diversity and inclusion professionals in corporate America, the IAT therefore seemed a perfect tool to deliver impartial results that make leaders aware of their own biases. It appeared to present a simple solution to a pernicious problem. Surely, the logic went, if we've learned that we have biases, none of us will ever act on them.

In hindsight, it's not surprising that this sentiment hasn't held up. After all, if awareness of bias was enough to mitigate it, orchestras would no longer need to hold blind auditions. Just inform the judges of the Boston Symphony Orchestra's lack of diversity, give them the IAT so they understand that they too are biased, then let them judge male and female musicians openly. No screens would be needed.

But of course, orchestras still hold blind auditions. Awareness of bias isn't enough to stop it.

BIAS TRAINING HASN'T LIVED UP TO ITS PROMISE

For businesses that have invested heavily in unconscious bias training, the impact of their efforts remains unproven. A 2009 study concluded that the causal effect of interventions such as bias training is unknown.[17] A 2017 article offered evidence that unconscious bias training is ineffectual, and it also suggested a reason: there's no proof that managers *act* on their unconscious bias.[18] There is, in other words, no demonstrated correlation between measures of unconscious bias such as the IAT and actual decision-making behavior in the workplace.

A problematic assumption may derive from this training's fundamental axiom: that it's possible to teach or convince individuals to resist their own biases on a consistent basis. But that idea doesn't account for the culture and processes that govern behavior and that might themselves be biased. In his 2011 book *Thinking, Fast and Slow*, Daniel Kahneman, Nobel laureate in economics, introduced the world to a well-established insight from psychological research that also makes intuitive sense: people don't have the time to think carefully about every decision that they make.

For only a few decisions do we engage in "slow" thinking, which involves logical analysis, the conscious application of rules, and a great deal of effort. For most decisions, a lack of time obliges us to rely on "fast" thinking: snap judgments based on intuition, habit, long-held beliefs, and stereotypes. This fast thinking, which is inevitable in most of our daily lives, is largely unconscious, so it's also inevitable that our unconscious biases will enter into it.[19]

Asking individuals to fix their own biases fails, as a standalone intervention, to address systemic pressures that reward "fast thinking" or "gut" decision-making, pressures that ensure current leadership archetypes remain in place.

When we interact with another person, whether as a coworker, subordinate, supervisor, or interviewee, we make countless "fast" decisions and judgments that add up to our opinion of that person. It's impossible to expect people to constantly call out their own bias, accurately note it, and appropriately compensate for it throughout an hour-long interview or promotion committee meeting, much less throughout the months or years that make up a working relationship.

"We were going to invest more in unconscious bias training since it had become such a common practice and most employees do value it," Maria Stolfi, global head of inclusion and engagement at Swiss Re, tells us. "But when we researched further, we found it's not proven to show results. So instead of trying to change minds, we're focusing on changing behavior."

One study even suggests that, by targeting managers for remediation, bias training may encourage a backlash against the diversity agenda.[20] In our experience, many managers consider these programs a "politically correct" waste of time, a "special favor" to women and minorities, or an attempt to "police" their thoughts.

Meanwhile, the overrepresentation of white men persists in corporate leadership.[21] Gender representation in the top ranks of Fortune 500 companies has remained about the same since 2000,[22] and the numbers for minority executives aren't much better.

Women and minorities do occupy some mid-level leadership roles, but not anywhere near in proportion to their representation of college and advanced degree holders in the US. Women make up 47.8 percent of the workforce and earn 57 percent of college degrees. But they're only 39.2 percent of first/mid-level managers, 29.7 percent of senior management, and, at Fortune 500 companies, 4.8 percent of CEOs. Racial and ethnic minorities make up 37.7 percent of the workforce and earn 34 percent of college degrees. But they're only 23.2 percent of first/mid-level managers, 14.0 percent of senior management and, at Fortune 500 companies, 5 percent of CEOs.[23]

With evidence that diversity training programs, generally based on the IAT, are at best a first step, we believe that there's a need for additional interventions, ones that look at areas that bias awareness training neglects.

BIAS TRAINING HAS A BLIND SPOT

It's something we've heard anecdotally from many of the companies with which we collaborate: *Okay, we're all aware that we're biased now, but so what? Nothing here has changed.* "Unconscious bias training raises awareness," says Seema Kumar, vice president of innovation, global health, and policy communication at Johnson & Johnson. "Following it up with comprehensive solutions can help to minimize bias and maximize inclusion."

The IAT and related trainings focus on managers who harbor bias. It's easy to see why organizations choose this focus: managers and leaders are the ones making hiring, firing, and promotion decisions, and they are in the position to see potential and grant opportunities to the employees who report to them. In short, they have the power.

Yet focusing on those who hold unconscious biases doesn't allow us to understand how bias is actually showing up in a company day to day. A manager who, according to the IAT or another such measure, harbors a host of biases may or may not act upon them in the workplace.[24] There's no study linking IAT scores or unconscious bias training programs with improvements in diversity or in organizations' bottom lines.

Despite a fortune spent on IATs and related trainings, most organizations don't know where bias happens or how much it costs.

Companies do have ways of tracking how employees experience bias and discrimination. Many offer channels—human resources, hotlines, ombudsmen—for employees to report such experiences. Yet these channels are usually disparate, scattershot, and primarily geared toward legal protection for the company. They do not offer a robust dataset from which to analyze bias's true cost or find effective solutions to remediate or mitigate it.

IN SEARCH OF SOLUTIONS THAT WORK

What would an effective solution consist of? The answer, we posit, is not to expect every individual to successfully identify and mitigate every possible instance of unconscious bias that they may exhibit. Instead, we identify conditions that cool down bias where it counts the most—when employees feel misjudged by leaders on their potential to succeed.

With its blind auditions, the Boston Symphony Orchestra didn't discover a way to get audition judges to recognize and compensate for all of their biases. It found a system that prevented those biases from influencing their judgment.

Unfortunately, for most decisions being made in corporate America, there's no way to create the equivalent of a blind audition. For internal promotions, anonymity isn't possible or even desirable, as subjective factors about an individual's performance and potential (which we'll explore below) are an important consideration when identifying future leaders in an annual review. And, of course, supervisors anoint leaders with everyday rewards, deciding who has the opportunity to *demonstrate* high performance and potential. Here, too, anonymity is impossible.

One of our interviewees, a healthcare executive whom we'll call Sandy,* reports that at her firm, people of color such as herself almost always choose not to put photos on their profiles in the company system. "It's our attempt to increase the odds that we'll be considered for a position," she says. "But we all know that it doesn't help that much."

In most organizations, the solution set will have to be more complex than putting up a screen and asking applicants to take off their shoes. It will have to target both manager behavior and the culture that shapes the employee experience. And it first requires research to understand precisely where bias is felt, so that organizations can map, measure, and disrupt it where costs to individuals and their organizations are the greatest.

---

* Throughout the text, the use of only a first name indicates that the name has been changed to ensure the source's anonymity.

With the goal of rethinking bias interventions by focusing on those who experience bias rather than those who harbor it, we built our project around four steps:

✓ *Codify assessments of employee potential*
In consultation with human resources and talent management experts, identify the key areas where bias creeps into decisions and judgments about employees.

✓ *Map where bias is perceived*
Survey white-collar employees about their perception of bias in the codified areas. With the results, create a heat map to illustrate who perceives bias in which area. Conduct focus groups and interviews to gather further insights.

✓ *Measure the costs*
Examine correlations between bias and employees' likelihood of behaviors that pose specific costs to organizations.

✓ *Identify how to disrupt bias*
Determine organizational interventions that correlate with a reduced likelihood of employees perceiving bias at work.

"There is something truly insurgent in saying, 'Hey, let's go look at the people who are impacted by bias, listen to them, and then figure out solutions based on that,' instead of starting top-down," Philippe Krakowsky, executive vice president and chief talent and strategy officer at Interpublic Group Mediabrands, told us after we shared our methodology with him. "In the past, we've known bias exists, we've known that it permeates institutions, and yet we've approached it in a way that is very process-oriented—and not very connected to its effects on the individual."

In the rest of this book, we'll first explain our procedure in detail, then present our results and conclusions.

2

Assessing Potential

"My current boss says openly that she thinks Latin Americans are lazy, disorganized, and irresponsible," says Luciana, a South American–born software developer at a global technology giant. "In my previous position here, I was leading a team of one hundred sixty developers to complete a project for a major client in the financial services industry. And I know that the client was satisfied. Now, my boss makes clear that she doesn't think I'm able to lead a project."

Luciana, who has two children and for years worked at her current company partly from home—with her team, clients, and supervisors spread out all over the world, there's little practical advantage to holding a video or telephone conference in the office—now finds that her flexible schedule is held against her.

"Before, no one cared what hours I was in the office, so long as the job got done on time and the client was happy. Suddenly, with my new boss, the fact that I work from home most days is considered a sign that I'm a lazy Latina," she says. With her children now older, Luciana is ready to seek new opportunities to fulfill a long-held ambition to move up into management. She's even eager to put in more face time at the office so that she can network more effectively.

"But my boss doesn't invite me to meetings," Luciana says. "She doesn't give me anyone to supervise. I'm lucky that she even lets me write code. If I turn in work early, she says nothing. If there is a delay, she announces that it's my fault, even if the cause is that the client changed requirements at the last minute and no one could have made the adjustments within the original deadline. Until this latest boss, I loved this company and was hoping to stay here forever. Now I don't have a chance here. I'm leaving as soon as I can."

Our first decision was to focus not on the moment when supervisors, HR departments, or hiring committees make a final decision about who gets a job or a promotion, but rather on what leads up to those decisions: assessments of employee potential.

Do your supervisors consider you to have potential? If they do, then they'll listen to your ideas and act on them. They'll give you plum assignments and clients. They'll cite your accomplishments when speaking to other managers. They'll put you on the right teams, assign you the best mentors, and give you chances to gain leadership experience. They'll let you know of opportunities before anyone else hears of them. They'll publicly praise you for success. If you express ambition, they'll compliment you for having goals. If you make a mistake, they'll protect you and call it a "teachable moment," because everyone makes mistakes now and then. They will, in sum, groom you to rise to the top.

"There are certain people in this organization, we call them the 'golden boys,'" a Latina vice president at a New York financial services company tells us. "They can't do anything wrong. Or rather, if they do something wrong, no one cares. They're all men with a similar background to the CEO and the rest of the C-suite. Funny how that happened."

If you aren't a "golden boy" or girl, you may come up with good ideas, but no one will listen. You may make important contributions, but no one important will notice. Even more likely, without the opportunities that certain clients and assignments provide, and without the encouragement, advice, and safety net that come with having a supportive supervisor, you'll never get the opportunity or confidence to take risks and come up with great ideas or make important contributions. If you express ambition, you'll be labeled pushy or impatient. And if you ever make a mistake, your supervisor will just consider it confirmation of what they had always expected.

Then, when that position you crave opens up, it won't matter if the process of awarding that promotion is as close to bias-free as humanly possible. Since you have been unfairly assessed for months or years, and had your opportunities limited, you won't have the strongest case. It will be an easy, obvious decision to give the position to your coworker, whom supervisors have judged so favorably and given so many opportunities to over the years.

How do supervisors judge their reports' potential? It's a highly subjective exercise, in part because what makes up potential isn't always well-defined, and in part because many of these assessments take place outside of annual performance reviews. They also take place in the thousands of on-the-spot decisions leading up to those annual reviews. Every day, week, and month, managers make decisions about which tasks, clients, projects, and resources are assigned to a given team member. And every day, week, and month they make judgments, often unconscious, about everything from that person's performance to their attitude and appearance.

"People pick up on bias when they see opportunities handed to colleagues for unclear reasons," Kate Burke, head of human capital and chief talent officer at AllianceBernstein, says. "They'll ask, 'Why did *that* person get the best account, the best region?' The manager's likely thinking, 'Who will connect best with that client base?' But that's where unfounded assumptions come in."

Lifetime career outcomes are the culmination of momentary assessments of individual potential—assessments that usually depend on subjective assumptions, a ripe breeding ground for bias. And with this "process" so full of possibilities for bias to enter, the odds rise that organizations are failing to give the best employees the best opportunities, leading to wasted (and demoralized) talent.

The first step of our strategic approach to disrupt bias is therefore to crack open that black box of assessments of employee potential.

INSIDE THE BLACK BOX: CODIFYING POTENTIAL

To root out bias in judgments of potential, we first need to codify how potential is assessed. To face the challenge of quantifying subjective assessments, we began with the experts: thirty-four human resource officers and diversity specialists.

When we solicited the ways in which these experts assess potential, certain phrases and themes appeared again and again, converging on the six most salient criteria that enter into assessments of employee potential:

- **Ability.** In this context, ability is an assessment of whether someone is competent and a fast learner, capable of taking on new responsibilities even if they haven't formally prepared for them. Unfortunately, when leaders assess someone's potential ability, a prestigious college degree often plays a disproportionate role.

- **Ambition.** A colleague's eagerness to take on additional responsibilities and expanded roles can be described in many ways. "Driven" and "goal-oriented" are positive. "Pushy," "demand-ing," and "overeager" are negative. But they may all describe the same behavior—and the latter words might imply some bias.

- **Commitment.** Dedication to a project's comple-tion and to overall company success is crucial for an individual who aspires to be a leader. But indi-viduals' managers can wrongly infer potential com-mitment from face time or weekly hours clocked.

- **Connections.** Employees involved in esteemed organizations or social circles inside or outside the workplace will likely be perceived as having relationships that benefit the business and make them more effective leaders. Yet others may have higher quality or deeper connections that can also provide business value—which might fly under the radar with their managers.

- **Emotional intelligence (EQ).** Employees who sense what others need from them and modify interactions accordingly are likely to be seen as having self-awareness, cultural awareness, and appreciation for difference. Assumptions can be made erroneously about emotional intelligence along lines of gender, sexual orientation, and ethnicity.

- **Executive presence (EP).** To merit promotion, leaders need the bearing to show they can make decisions and drive followership at the next level.

But individuals who look, sound, and act like current company leaders may be seen as having EP potential for the wrong reasons.

We call these six criteria (Ability, Ambition, Commitment, Connections, Emotional Intelligence, Executive Presence) the ACE model. These criteria may be important for defining an employee's potential and chances of advancement, but the process of judging whether an employee has them or not is hardly objective. This subjectivity leaves room for bias to creep in. But how can we quantify this bias?

It might seem like an impossible task. But unless bias is quantified, it will be difficult to fight. And it will be nearly impossible to judge how well that fight is succeeding. Fortunately, our new lens on bias offers a way to measure bias and correlate that measurement with costs to the organization.

WITH BIAS, PERCEPTION IS REALITY

Several years ago, Maya, a management consulting executive, took a business trip in Switzerland. On a Swiss Rail train to catch her flight from Zurich to New York after a big client presentation, she was busy catching up on emails on her laptop and had her ticket out on her tray table, so the conductor could take it without interrupting her work as he came through the car.

The conductor had been swiftly moving through the train car, collecting tickets without much interaction with passengers, but when he arrived to scan Maya's ticket, he paused. He asked to see her passport. Maya retrieved her passport from her bag and handed it over. At the sight of her US passport, she thought, the conductor was visibly taken aback. It occurred to Maya, who is of South Asian descent, that it might be because she has brown skin.

The conductor flipped through the passport suspiciously, pausing at the many stamps—as a successful consultant, Maya frequently travels for international clients—until he reached the photo page. He glanced from the picture to Maya several times, then brusquely handed back the passport without a word and finally scanned her ticket.

Maya watched him as he proceeded down the aisle. He didn't pause at any other passenger, never mind ask for anyone else's passport. And everybody else on the train happened to be white.

Maya frequently reflects on this experience, which left her humiliated and angry. "It makes me feel small and so diminished," she says. "I have degrees from some of the most prestigious institutions in the world. But in Switzerland, I run the risk of being seen as 'less than' because of the color of my skin."

Maya can't know for certain whether the conductor was acting on his personal bias. Perhaps he was following some Swiss Rail protocol, such as checking the ID of every hundredth passenger. Perhaps Maya matched the description of a wanted criminal suspected to be riding the train that day.

But the real motives behind the conductor's actions hardly matter. Maya perceived racial bias, and the experience affected her in both the short and long term. For the rest of that train ride, anger distracted her from her work. And ever since, she's had a negative impression of Switzerland. When possible, Maya now tries to schedule meetings in neighboring countries and—since she's at a level at which she can pick and choose clients—she's occasionally turned down opportunities to work in Switzerland.

Experiences like Maya's are why we first decided to focus our study on employees' *perception* of bias. In Maya's case, this perception temporarily impacted her ability to work effectively and has for years impacted the way she views the entity (in this case, a country) that she believes treated her unfairly.

When it comes to its impact on employees' contributions—or costs to the organization—bias is in the eye of the beholder. Employees who believe that they're not getting a fair shake are more likely to burn out, quit, or even sabotage their employers. In other words, with bias, perception is reality.

Employees' perception of bias is thus not just a way to identify where bias is likely taking place and interfering with the correct assessment and advancement of employees. Perception of bias is, whether accurate or not, a destructive force in itself. And as we'll see in the last part of this book, focusing on the perception of bias allows for a new approach to remediation and mitigation that invites collaboration—not defensiveness—from managers.

"Pointing out how employees perceive bias is very different from pointing out bias in managers," says Robert Dibble, managing director and Americas head of human resources at Deutsche Bank. "You're not saying, 'Here's what you've done.' You're saying, 'This is what people perceive.' It precludes a combative or defensive response. That's critical when you're trying to change managers' behavior."

UNDERSTANDING BIAS

With the ACE model for assessments of employee potential as our basis, we wanted to understand how employees perceive bias. Do they think that their current supervisors are fairly assessing their potential? Or do they see bias in their supervisors' judgment of them?

We set out to answer these questions in a nationally representative survey of 3,570 full-time, college-educated employees in white-collar jobs between the ages of twenty-one and sixty-five. Of those, 1,918 were at large companies, defined as having one thousand or more employees. This large-company sample—on which all of the graphics and findings below are based—included 907 men and 1,011 women. For a deeper dive on our methodology, please see page 137.

We asked survey respondents a series of questions to elicit two pieces of information about each ACE element: how they judge themselves, and how they believe their supervisors judge them. We ascertained the latter by asking them about feedback they've received and what they believe that their supervisors think of them.

For each ACE category, we divided respondents into two categories. The first were those who reported that their superiors' assessment of them is equal to, or better than, their self-assessment. These individuals don't perceive negative bias. The second category were those respondents who reported that their superiors assess them more negatively than they assess themselves. We deduced that these individuals perceive bias.

In other words, if an employee rates herself highly on one or more of the ACE categories, and if she believes that her supervisors rate her poorly in that category, then we infer that she considers herself to be incorrectly judged. She believes that she's suffered bias. For example, if you're highly committed to your work and career, but you say that your supervisors don't recognize this fact—perhaps because you're on a flex schedule or have recently returned from a leave of absence—then you consider your commitment incorrectly assessed. You perceive bias in this ACE category.

PART TWO
WHERE BIAS AFFLICTS ORGANIZATIONS

3

Mapping Bias

Carl has autism spectrum disorder, and while that creates social difficulties, he's able to function at a high level at his job in finance. But his start was difficult. He began his career with a summer internship, where he disclosed his disability. However, he soon found that his first boss wasn't treating him like the other newly recruited graduates. "He sent everyone else in my group each afternoon for tasks and experiences in different parts of the building. He told me to stay where I was and cover for the receptionist, who was on vacation. He was supposed to be preparing us for management roles. He wasn't preparing me." Carl, whose disability makes it especially difficult for him to confront such situations, just kept his head down and did as he was told.

On the second rotation of his internship, Carl had a different boss. This one sat him down and said, "I hope this isn't too awkward, but tell me about your disability. What are your limitations and needs? If there's anything you can't do or need help doing, would you feel comfortable telling me about it?" Carl informed this new boss that he really didn't have any limitations or needs. But the conversation meant the world to Carl, who knew his manager cared about his success. Four years later, Carl is thriving at the company.

Which employees are most likely to report that their superiors misjudge their potential? Which aspects of the ACE model are most often perceived to be misjudged? To better understand the perception and impact of bias, we organized our data findings into a heat map (see opposite page) that shows which talent cohorts in large companies are more likely (black) or less likely (light gray) to perceive bias in each ACE competency. Those farther to the right, on the darker, hotter side of the map, are more likely to perceive negative bias on two or more categories—in that case, we infer that they perceive "ACE bias." Those least likely to report ACE bias are at the far left, on the lighter, cooler gray side.

EXPECTED AND UNEXPECTED FINDINGS

The heat map confirms many traditional hypotheses around bias and diversity. For instance, black, Latino, and Asian cohorts are more likely to report ACE bias than white cohorts. Employees with disabilities—a group for which exclusion is well documented[25]—are on the far right of the heat map, along with employees born outside of the US.

But several of our findings were counterintuitive. For example, in our sample, men are more likely to report ACE bias than women, and Asians are more likely to report ACE bias than blacks or Latinos.

EMPLOYEES AT LARGE COMPANIES who perceive negative bias in their superiors' assessment of ACE elements

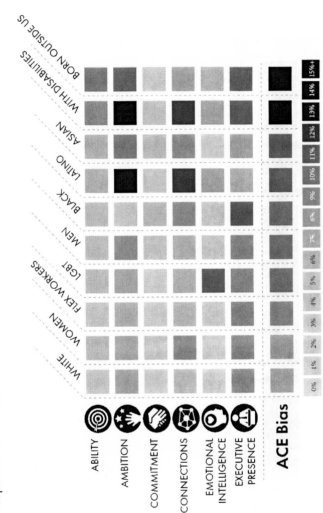

These surprising findings may be of particular value to organizations seeking to mitigate the costs bias imposes on them by creating dissatisfied and, in some cases, angry employees. For example, the findings may lead organizations to implement interventions aimed at mitigating the bias and frustration that many Asians— who are not always viewed as a group that suffers bias— experience when they aim for leadership positions.

Counterintuitive findings may also indicate a need to look at the data more closely, as we'll do in the chapters that follow. For now, we'll focus on the most important factor in how bias afflicts organizations: which employees *perceive* bias, and in which categories.

INTERPRETING THE PREVALENCE OF ACE BIAS

The percentage of employees in each talent cohort who perceive ACE bias ranges from 7.7 percent to 14.5 percent, with an average of 9.2 percent. At first glance, these numbers may seem low. But in our survey, we didn't ask about lifetime experiences of bias in general. We asked about a very specific kind of bias— involving assessments of potential—that employees are perceiving from supervisors at their current companies. A 9.2-percent rate of ACE bias means that if you're a manager at a large company with eleven people on your team, the odds are that one of your team members perceives this kind of bias right now. And when faced with some manager behaviors or leadership teams, the rates can rise above 20 percent for some talent cohorts, as we'll see in Part Four of this book.

This level of bias carries significant costs. Employees at large companies who perceive ACE bias are, over the past year, 32 percent less likely to have received a raise, 45 percent less likely to have had their job responsibilities increased, 41 percent less likely to have received career development opportunities, and 25 percent less likely to have received a promotion compared to those who do not perceive ACE bias.

They're also, as we'll see in Part Three, much more likely than their peers who don't perceive bias to disengage from work, keep innovative ideas to themselves, look for employment elsewhere, or even actively sabotage the company and its brand. The hunt for new markets (including abroad and among diverse populations), the need for innovation, the competition for talent, and the value of branding are also more important to their bottom lines than ever. The cost of having many of your employees *not* on your side in these areas, as well as in their daily tasks, is great.

We'll explore in detail bias's cost to organizations and data-driven solutions in Part Three and Part Four. For now, we'll take a more granular look at our data and explore the experiences of some of the talent cohorts most likely to perceive ACE bias.

4

Global Talent at Risk

Julio, who was born and raised in a small Caribbean country, is the head of technology at a global advertising firm's office in a major US city. It's a good job and he's good at it. But it's looking to be a dead end, and he's convinced that the reason is bias.

Julio wants to be head of the firm's technology operations not just for one city, but for all of North America. He's sure that he can handle the position. In fact, he's already doing most of the work, since his boss has given him responsibility for technology operations in four other major cities. And the position he craves is currently vacant.

But when Julio went to speak to his boss to find out what he had to do to get the role, his boss told him to forget about it. He couldn't come up with any concrete reason why Julio should give up on his ambition. He just said, "We think you're more of a do-er than a manager type, so we'd like to keep you doing more yourself, instead of managing more people."

"But I'm already managing people," Julio tells us. "I'm managing people here and in four other cities. I was just hired for one city, then I did well enough that they gave me the other cities to manage too, so how can I not be a manager type? It doesn't make any sense. It has to be bias."

As our heat map on page 31 shows, employees in our sample born outside the US like Julio are the most likely to perceive ACE bias (14.5 percent). When we further break down the data by region, we see that the talent cohort that most often reports ACE bias (19.7 percent) are employees born in Latin America.

Let's go back to Julio, who went to college in his home country, not an Ivy League school as most of his firm's senior management did. As a result, he's not a part of "old boy" networks and he has the sense that his superiors look down on his degree. To Julio, that's an unfair disadvantage, but he accepts it as somewhat inevitable. Another kind of bias frustrates him more. Twice he was asked not to give presentations to clients on technology whose development he had personally overseen because account executives said Julio "might not make a good impression" or "get along so well with these guys."

Well-spoken and fluent in English after more than a decade in the US, Julio has extensive experience with client presentations. "But I still speak with an accent, and I'm from the Caribbean, so I don't look and sound the way people here expect a tech guy to."

EMPLOYEES BORN OUTSIDE the US who perceive negative bias in their superiors' assessment of their...

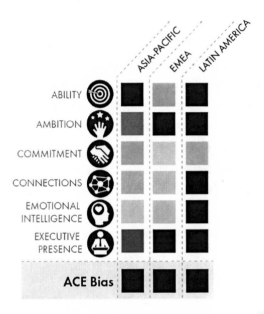

Unfortunately, Julio is experiencing the three most prevalent types of bias for executives born in Latin America: he feels his ambition, connections, and emotional intelligence are all underestimated. He knows that he's not being considered for the position he wants. He's certain that it's harder for him than US-born executives to build a network inside his firm, an experience that CTI's prior research has shown is common: among foreign-born Latinos, 44 percent say they have to work harder than their peers to feel included.[26]

Adriana Ocampo, a planetary geologist and science program manager at NASA, has felt the sting of ACE bias. She is one of the scientists credited with discovering the Chicxulub impact crater, a ring almost two hundred kilometers wide under the Yucatán peninsula that is believed to be the site of the asteroid collision that wiped out the dinosaurs sixty-six million years ago.[27] With geo-archeologist Kevin Pope, Ocampo published her findings in the scientific journal *Nature* in 1991, ahead of other teams with geologic evidence that likewise pointed to the connection. But to this day, she says, people in the scientific community refuse to accept that she published first.

A native of Colombia, she completed her PhD in planetary geology at the Vrije Universiteit in Amsterdam—but she wasn't well-connected among *Nature*'s peer review committee. "People said, 'We have never heard of you and you have come now to say that you have found a crater that the whole [peer review] committee has been looking for?'" She struggled for months to get her research published. When *Nature* finally published the article, they required that she put a question mark in its title.

Latin Americans may have the greatest level of frustration as they seek to rise to the top, but they aren't the only foreign-born employees to perceive significant bias in US companies.

Consider Anjali, who sits in the highest levels of corporate America. She's on the board of directors of a Fortune 500 financial services company and on the board of a publicly traded asset management giant. But for a few years, her path to the top looked to be blocked by bias.

Anjali came to the US from India for an MBA, then found a job at a management consulting firm. She was putting up excellent numbers, but the news came that her department head was receiving requests that she be reassigned. The requests had nothing to do with her analytical skills or the content of the advice she was giving. Instead, several clients, especially in Southern states, simply didn't like working with her. Despite being brought in as a consultant precisely to shake up companies and turn them around, they said that she was "too aggressive" or "too pushy" and "made them uncomfortable."

"I didn't do or say anything that my colleagues didn't," Anjali says. "I think that they had trouble with a woman with brown skin and an Indian accent asking them hard questions about how they were running their businesses. From a US-born man, those questions were considered assertive and to-the-point. From me, they were seen as pushy."

Anjali's experience is all too common among Asian-born individuals, who report significant bias around assessments of their ability (12.0 percent) and executive presence (9.5 percent). In some professions, the two biases intersect: bias around Anjali's executive presence made her own firm's management view her as less able to do her job advising clients.

Anjali says that she learned to make adjustments to make a better impression, and that these adjustments were a good experience for her. She also says that it's the responsibility of immigrants like her to learn the codes of US society and business. "We have to work harder to fit in," she says. "That's part of being an immigrant." But she worries that American businesses will be putting themselves at a disadvantage if they don't make themselves more welcoming of foreign-born executives.

"The competition for top talent is global and it's intense," she says. "American companies just can't afford to drive away top performers with bias."

5

The Curse of the "Model Minority"

"Before I came to ESPN, which has given me great opportunities, I encountered a lot of what I call 'place-ism,' meaning, 'know your place,'" says Mike Huang, deputy editor in charge of NBA content for ESPN's online initiatives in China. "The message a lot of Asian men get is, 'Hey, you're good at crunching numbers, great, but don't try to get into the operational side.'"

Huang, a self-described extrovert, has seen himself as a leader ever since he was elected captain of his high school (and then college) football team. He doesn't fit the personality stereotype—nor, at 6'2", 250 pounds, the physical stereotype—often applied to Asian men in the corporate world. "It's important for Asians to learn self-promotion so that their skills and ambition are recognized," he says. "But it's also important for management to learn to see talent beneath different cultural expressions."

Among employees of color that we surveyed, Asians are the most likely to perceive ACE bias. On assessments of ambition, for example, Asian men in our sample are 52 percent more likely than white men to report being misjudged.

These results surprised us. We had hypothesized that black or Latino employees would be more likely to report ACE bias, in part because of the "model minority" moniker applied to men and women of Asian heritage in the US.

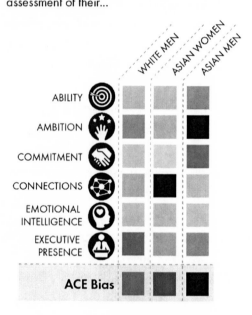

EMPLOYEES AT LARGE COMPANIES who perceive negative bias in their superiors' assessment of their...

The myth of Asians as a "model minority" has been around for decades. In 1966, an article in *The New York Times Magazine* called "Success Story, Japanese-American Style" praised Japanese Americans' success despite wartime discrimination and attributed it to their values, work ethic, and family structure.[28] Since then, the assumption that Asians are more likely to achieve academic success, especially in math and science, has persisted. It's a stereotype that's misleading, since it hides massive differences in wealth and academic achievement inside Asian-American communities.[29] It's a stereotype which has been and continues to be used to pit Asian Americans against other minority groups.[30] It's a stereotype that fuels an assumption that Asians are likely to have overcome all obstacles to advancement, when that's far from the truth.[31] And it's a stereotype that may help fuel an unwarranted assumption that Asians are likely to be "nerds."[32]

Several of our interviewees and focus group participants reported how the "model minority" myth can be a double-edged sword. The assumption that they lack interpersonal skills, some Asian men say, hurts them more than their supposed mathematical talents help them when they're seeking not just to work as engineers or analysts, but to rise into leadership positions.

Multiple Asian respondents in our focus groups said that their companies' top management consider Asian employees "too technical to be promoted to management," or "only good at technical roles, not at leadership roles," or "unwilling or unable to lead, except maybe other Asians."

Interestingly, Asian men we surveyed are more likely than Asian women to perceive this bias around ambition (12.0 percent vs. 5.4 percent). Similarly, more Asian men than women in our sample (8.2 percent vs. 4.6 percent) report bias in assessments of their ability.

Jane Hyun, global leadership coach, author of *Breaking the Bamboo Ceiling* and coauthor of *Flex*, says being seen as a "tech wizard" can be a trap for some Asian men. "If the stereotype is that, as an Asian male, you are assumed to have strong quantitative skills, and you mess up an analysis, then the penalty may be greater because the expectation was much higher to begin with," she says.

There may also be a cultural reason why so many Asian men report bias around how their ability and ambition are assessed. White managers, Mike Huang says, might perceive their Asian reports and colleagues as not particularly ambitious or able, because many simply do the job they're asked to do, then go home without comment. "We're taught not to brag about ourselves," Mike Huang says. "We're taught to just go and work. That's how my dad raised me. He would tell me, 'Just shut your mouth and do your work.'"

Ankit is another Asian man who, early in his career, faced bias over his ambition. A few years after completing his MBA, he took a job at a leading management consulting firm. He had excellent reviews, but unlike his white colleagues, he wasn't getting leadership assignments. Without those assignments, he knew he stood little chance of receiving a promotion, and if he didn't get promoted, the firm's "up-or-out" policy meant that he might lose his job.

An Indian American, Ankit is tall and well-built, speaks like the New Yorker he is, and loves to play and talk sports. So he didn't think that cultural differences were holding him back. "My assumption was that it was about the color of my skin."

Finally Ankit was assigned to a project whose leader worried him from the start. "I just had a feeling that he didn't like Asians or anyone who looked different from him. He was a real good old boy type." Sure enough, even though Ankit did his customary good work, this supervisor gave him his first-ever poor review in the firm, even though the review didn't actually cite any weaknesses in Ankit's performance. Furious at the injustice, Ankit went to his firm's ombudsman. "I told him, 'Compare this review to every other review I've gotten. Look at how few specifics this one has. Do you really think I'd suddenly stop doing good work?'"

The ombudsman got Ankit a meeting with the CEO, who looked at the many good reviews Ankit had gotten, as well as his persistent failure to receive a leadership assignment. He agreed that Ankit had been suffering bias and made sure his next assignment was as a project leader.

"That company had a great ombudsman and CEO, and I was willing to fight for myself," Ankit says. "But what happens in companies that don't have such good awareness among top management, or with people who may have cultural issues around speaking up?"

Some people assume Asian women have difficulty speaking up as well, which may interfere with their capacity to build networks in their workplaces. When others assume they're bad at building relationships, it can be hard to break the ice—or change others' minds. Fully 15.3 percent of Asian women report bias in our "connections" category.

Eunice, a Korean-American surgeon at a teaching hospital in the Midwest, reports that she's often gotten feedback that she's "timid" and "hard to get to know." Since she describes herself as "polite and friendly," she believes that this assessment of her is incorrect and based on stereotypes. "Everyone thinks that Asian women are shy, even though I'm not." Yet she does say that she feels at a disadvantage when it comes to networking. "You have to promote yourself, but I'm bad at that. In my parents' culture, self-promotion isn't seen as a virtue. It's arrogance."

She adds that many people in the hospital treat her and the one other Asian-American surgeon (who is Chinese, not Korean) interchangeably, confusing their names and assuming that they have the same specialty (they don't). "It's hard to network when people think that every Asian woman is the same," she says.

Cultural issues around speaking up and demanding one's rights aren't limited to Asians. As we'll see, they may help explain another one of our surprising findings—that black women we surveyed perceive bias less often than black or Asian men.

6

Paying the "Black Tax" in Silence

We had hypothesized that black women would perceive more bias than men of color. After all, in past research, we've found black women are highly ambitious, yet struggle to break through to leadership ranks. Our report *Black Women: Ready to Lead* found that black women are 2.8 times as likely as white women to aspire to powerful positions with prestigious titles. They're also more likely than white women (43 percent vs. 30 percent) to express confidence that they can succeed in positions of power.[33]

Though they are more likely to perceive ACE bias than white women (9.8 percent vs. 6.4 percent), black women we surveyed are less likely to report ACE bias than black men (11.2 percent), Asian men (12.1 percent), or Latino men (12.4 percent). In other words, black women are more likely to see alignment between their own sense of career potential and their superiors' assessments of their potential. They are less likely to perceive bias, even though they are also highly underrepresented (as we discussed in Part One) in leadership positions.

EMPLOYEES AT LARGE COMPANIES who perceive negative bias in their superiors' assessment of their...

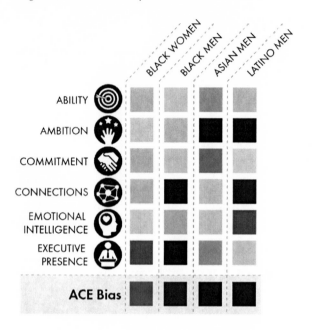

What's behind this surprising result? Our interviews and research offer some theories—neither of them conclusive.

TEMPERED EXPECTATIONS

Six years ago, Kimberly, now a vice president in the marketing department of a global healthcare company, applied for a promotion as a middle manager while still working at another healthcare company. The position she wanted demanded both client-facing skills and networks on which to build a book of business. She would "own" a particular customer portfolio, and act as liaison between the customer and company. She had excellent results and the right experience, but she was turned down.

"My supervisor was direct. She said, 'You didn't get the position because of where you come from.'"

Kimberly was born and raised in an inner-city neighborhood where hardly anyone saw a future outside of menial work or crime. For a time, she was homeless. But Kimberly had worked her way through high school, college, and graduate school. She thought she'd moved on—until this conversation with her supervisor.

"When she said that to me, I almost lost my mind," she says. "It took me back to everything I'd dealt with as a child, where the constant message was that I wasn't any good, that I'd never amount to anything because I was from a poor, urban, African-American community."

At the time, Kimberly was too shocked to protest or demand a better explanation. She didn't take the matter to senior management or even look for another job, though it was clear that she'd never rise at her current company. "I was just too depressed," she said. "I didn't think I'd get anything else."

Kimberly describes what appears to be a common phenomenon among black women: low expectations. If they are less likely to report ACE bias on average than men of color, it may not be because they suffer less bias. Instead, resigned to navigating a system that is anything but meritocratic, they often fail to perceive negative bias from managers because poor treatment is what they've been raised to accept as normal.

This resignation may be an outgrowth of behavioral psychology wherein individuals endure damaging situations rather than attempt to escape them. They have learned from previous experience that nothing they do will change the outcome; in the words of one study of black women, "Higher education and income do not appear to protect women from experiencing racism and feeling hopeless or powerless in response."[34]

When she spoke about this incident in our interview, Kimberly recognized that she'd suffered bias, but she said that she'd never told anyone except her husband about it before. "It never occurred to me to tell anyone," she says.

She now hopes to work her way into senior management at her current company, but she says with a shrug that the odds are stacked against her. "I just know that I'm going to have to work twice as hard as anyone else under consideration. That's just the way it is."

BLINDSIDED

Past research we've conducted at CTI suggests another explanation for the low incidence of ACE bias among black women.[35] Ambitious black women rate themselves highly. They also believe that their supervisors assess them highly, but that's because they're missing the most important element to understand how their supervisors are thinking: constructive feedback. Only 11 percent of black women have sponsors, and in many cases, our interviewees tell us, their sponsors—especially if they aren't also people of color—hesitate to tell them when they're poorly assessed.[36]

Tiffany, a marketing executive at a pharmaceutical firm, recalls her shock and dismay the first time she received a negative performance review—twelve years into her career. "When I'd asked for constructive criticism on my presentations, everyone told me I was doing just fine," Tiffany recalls. "In fact, I'd been handed every promotion I asked for."

Then she got a new manager, who told Tiffany that she didn't have the client management skills or leadership presence to move up to the next level at the company. At first, the news was difficult for Tiffany to hear in her end-of-year review. She was so upset, she threatened to quit.

But over the holidays, she pondered the feedback and decided that it had merit. When she returned to work in the New Year, she pulled her manager aside. "If you would work with me," Tiffany said, "I would very much like to work with you to develop as a leader and get to the next level."

With that meeting began an extraordinary alliance. Tiffany's manager started giving her opportunities to work with clients and colleagues, as well as continuous, detailed feedback. In short, though her firm didn't have a formal sponsorship program, Tiffany had a sponsor. Today, Tiffany is head of her firm's marketing department. If she hadn't started to receive honest and negative feedback, Tiffany doesn't think she would be the leader she is today.

Kimberly's and Tiffany's stories are two sides of the same coin: Kimberly didn't react to a poor assessment because she didn't know what she could do about it; Tiffany didn't react to poor assessments because she didn't know that she was receiving them.

But even if black women in our sample are less likely to perceive ACE bias than men of color, they are aware that something is wrong. Earlier CTI research shows that 44 percent of black women report "feeling stalled" in their careers, as opposed to 30 percent of white women.[37]

7

Assertive, Angry, or Both?

Max is a star in the ad world, a man who might already be at the very top of his firm—if he were white. A creative director and vice president at a major agency, he's had award-winning campaigns. He's brought in new accounts worth millions. He began and led his firm's rapid growth into digital and interactive advertising. He leads the agency's second largest account. And now he's utterly disillusioned with his company, because, despite receiving a raise recently, he says that his progression has been remarkably slow.

"It took me twice as long to make VP as my white colleagues," he says. "I have supervisors who can't lead their way out of a box, but they got where they are because they've had someone pushing for them. I've been here sixteen years, and I still don't have that."

Max believes that the fact that no one on the all-white senior management team is pushing for him, the lone black employee in his division, is not a coincidence. "I hate to say it," he says, "but it's bias. I look around and I can't see any other explanation."

In our sample, black men like Max are more likely than white men to perceive bias around their connections (13.7 percent vs. 5.6 percent) and executive presence (13.5 percent vs. 8.6 percent). It's hard to rise to the top in corporate America if you don't receive credit for the networks you have and if people don't see you as a leader.

EMPLOYEES AT LARGE COMPANIES
who perceive negative bias in their
superiors' assessment of their...

Max is certain that his background provides the company with benefits. He recently led his team to create a highly successful social media campaign based on a hip-hop video. To make it, he leaned on contacts he had inside and outside the agency. "But I got hardly any credit for it. I see white guys do far less for the agency and get celebrated. We won an award for that project, and I was the creative on it, so the team tells me to keep the trophy. But my boss comes over and says, 'I'm the executive creative director, that award is mine, not yours.' He didn't work at all on the project, he opposed it, and he also never says that kind of thing to anyone else. The next day, I'm in his office, someone asks about the award, he looks right at me says, 'Oh, that. It's just a paperweight.' It's the worst feeling in the world: to work so hard, and do good work, then not be recognized for it."

Like many other people of color, Max describes meetings where his ideas are simply passed over, then someone white says the same thing and receives attention and applause. Despite his successful initiation of the firm's digital growth strategy, and his continued emphasis on digital and interactive work on his own accounts, Max finds senior management never comes to him for insights into digital campaigns. "It's like I'm invisible," he says. "I've got great ideas I'm sitting on because I'm not convinced I'd get listened to, and I don't know if I'd get credit if I did. I'm certainly not going to take risks, because I know that if I mess up, it's hell on earth, while my white colleagues get a pass."

And he describes the paradox that this situation creates for black men who seek to establish themselves as leaders: if they fail to aggressively pitch their ideas and demand credit for them, no one will pay attention. But if they do push hard to lead with their ideas, they may not be seen as strong leaders. Instead, they risk getting labeled as "angry black men" who scare their white colleagues.

"If I were white, I wouldn't be seen as angry, I'd be seen as passionate," Max says. "But if I were white, I wouldn't have to fight so hard in the first place. Now I really have gotten angry."

Despite a salary that Max calls "very generous," he's finally looking for work in another agency. "I want to be someplace where I can just do good work and get credit for it and be listened to if I come up with a good idea. I'm tired of having to fight for everything."

Many black men in our focus groups report problems similar to Max's. "We're seen as physically intimidating," one man says, "so we have to be less assertive verbally." Another tells us that black men "can't afford to ever look upset. You're supposed to walk around smiling the whole time." A third describes attending a meeting with his boss, who praised his colleague (a small white woman) for her aggressive approach to clients and criticized him for not acting the same. "But I can't do that," he says. "I'm a six-foot-five black man. If I'm not always soft-spoken and polite, white people get scared of me."

A black woman who's an account executive at a public relations firm tells us that black men who start in her area always have to leave it if they want to rise.

"The firm never lets black men do client relations at a senior level. They always say 'chemistry's not right,' but what they mean is that they think that white men won't want to hear black men advise them on how to spend their money."

Research unfortunately confirms these anecdotes. Neuroscientists at New York University recently monitored brain activity with functional magnetic resonance imaging (fMRI) while showing individuals images of different races and genders expressing various emotions. Most subjects initially viewed black men as angry, even when their facial expressions were ones generally correlated with happiness. The same study found that women of all races were generally seen as happy, even when they displayed facial expressions meant to express anger.[38]

Black men aren't the only group for whom we uncovered indications of incorrect assessments that lead to genuine resentment. But the barriers that many Latinos perceive are slightly different.

8

"Too Lazy" *and* "Pushing Too Hard"

Carlos, an investment portfolio manager at an industrial conglomerate, has always seen himself on a turbocharged track for leadership. When he joined the company, he was a credit analyst. Three years later, he oversees multiple projects worth more than $100 million each. He also helps set overall strategy for the firm's billions in North American capital spending.

But a pair of recent linked experiences has led him to question whether he can expect to keep advancing.

The first warning bell went off at his midyear assessment last year. Carlos sat down with his supervisor and laid out his ambitions for his future at the company. He told his supervisor where he wanted to go, what he thought he needed to do, and what responsibilities he thought he needed to take on to get there. Then he asked his supervisor: Were these plans realistic? If not, what else should he consider?

The supervisor told Carlos that he shouldn't push so hard. "You need to tone down your approach, soften your delivery. Don't be so open about your ambitions."

Then he added, "Just keep doing the same things you've been doing, and you'll get there."

A few months later, Carlos was part of a panel interviewing an investment analyst candidate. The candidate, a white male, would have to relocate across the US to take the position. Carlos and the panel questioned him about his willingness to do that.

"He said he would relocate," Carlos says. "He told us he would do whatever it takes to get ahead. He explained to us how this position we were offering would be a useful stepping-stone for him on his way to a job in a different division of our company. He outlined precisely what his final goal was and what steps he needed to take, including a few years working with us, to get there."

When the panel met after the interview to discuss this candidate, Carlos expected his peers to comment unfavorably on the candidate's naked ambition. Instead, they praised it.

"They all said that it was great to see a man who articulates exactly where he wants to go and how he's going to get there. 'This is the kind of dynamic person that we need,' they said. I couldn't believe what I was hearing. But I kept quiet."

After this encounter, Carlos spent a lot of time reflecting on the difference between how he and the applicant had been treated. "There's this perception that Latinos are lazy and not as ambitious as others," he said. "But on the flip side, if you are ambitious like anyone else, it's perceived as overly aggressive."

EMPLOYEES AT LARGE COMPANIES
who perceive negative bias in their
superiors' assessment of their...

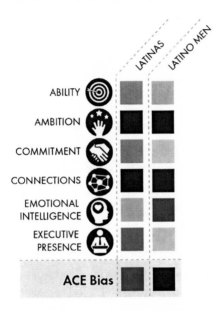

Our data shows that ambition is the dimension of the ACE model in which Latino men most often believe themselves to be incorrectly assessed: 14.8 percent report bias here, the highest number of any talent cohort. Latinas aren't far behind: 13.3 percent report bias over ambition.

At the same time, 10.8 percent of Latino men and 13.8 percent of Latinas perceive bias around connections. Isabela, a vice president at a New York bank, says that when promotions to a senior level are determined, "formal criteria go out the window. Top executives gather in a room and fight for their preferred candidates. By the time the formal assessment process begins, the decision has already been made." If you don't have a sponsor willing to fight for you, your odds of reaching senior management are zero, Isabela says, and she finds that it's harder for Latinas like her to find those sponsors. "There just aren't many people like me at the top. It's all very white here."

At the same time that they encounter bias when trying to form networks within senior management, many Latinos to whom we spoke in interviews and focus groups reported deep connections and networks in their communities, and, in some cases, ancestral countries that they say their employers fail to value. And as other CTI research shows, the tendency among Latinos to embrace their heritage and assert their roots is *growing* as millennials replace older generations in the workplace.[39]

"Latinos in the US are a market for us that's growing faster than the overall US market," a focus group participant says. "The kind of experience we have could really add to the success of the company, but they're not using it."

With their ambitions and networks underutilized, many Latinos are frustrated, though similar to blacks, Latino men are more likely to perceive bias than are Latinas. This difference between men and women persists among LGB colleagues.

9

ACE Bias and Sexual Orientation

Chris Thangaraj, a senior vice president for portfolio strategy and analytics for Bank of America, started off his career at a different bank on a very different path: client relations. He thought that he was good at it but soon realized, as an openly gay man, that he'd never get far in that field. His supervisors wouldn't assign him men as clients. They assigned him instead to the men's daughters, wives, and widows.

"My supervisors were pretty direct about it," Thangaraj says. "In performance reviews they said I'd have difficulties connecting with male clients, so they almost never gave me the chance." Instead, he says, client-facing roles went to stereotypical straight white men, often former college athletes, and some women. "The message given to me was that I either had to be in the closet or not have the same opportunities that my colleagues had," Thangaraj says. "So I left that area."

Gay or bisexual men are the most likely (14.9 percent) of all cohorts we surveyed to perceive bias in their superiors' assessment of their emotional intelligence, or EQ. Gay men in our focus groups concur that bias about their EQ has constrained their opportunities relative to their heterosexual colleagues. Supervisors, they say, assume that clients or reports will be homophobic. Or they assume that gay men won't be able to make conversation with straight men since (the assumption goes) gay men don't participate in sports or in family life.

EMPLOYEES AT LARGE COMPANIES
who perceive negative bias in their
superiors' assessment of their...

LGB WOMEN

GB MEN

ABILITY

AMBITION

COMMITMENT

CONNECTIONS

EMOTIONAL
INTELLIGENCE

EXECUTIVE
PRESENCE

ACE Bias

Fearing they will confront such bias can lead gay or bisexual men to behave in ways that in turn confirm managers' assumptions about their emotional intelligence, says Sonelius Kendrick-Smith, a director in the asset management division of Deutsche Bank.

To avoid bias, for example, gay or bisexual men may hide their sexual orientation or be constantly on the lookout for threats—behaviors that create obstacles to emotional connection. "The only way to build trust with others is for them to feel that you are authentic, honest, and open," Sonelius says. "You can't do that if you're hiding something, or if you're ashamed or frightened of something. People don't communicate well when their defenses are up."

In contrast, managers appear to have more favorable perceptions of lesbian, gay, or bisexual women's emotional intelligence: only 4.9 percent of LGB women report bias on this front. Counterbalancing stereotypes may explain it: perhaps because women are perceived as "naturally" emotionally intelligent, managers don't assume LGB women will have trouble connecting with male clients or straight team members.

Several lesbians whom we interviewed say that their sexual orientation sometimes levels the playing field in mostly male environments. "It's easier for me to be one of the guys and fit into a masculine environment like the trading floor," says Helena, a lesbian bond trader. "When an attractive woman walks by our desks, I have no problem joining in the conversation." Whether or not her behavior is appropriate in the workplace, it certainly does give her "in-group" status.

In fact, lesbian, gay, or bisexual women in our sample are the single *least* likely talent cohort to report: only 4.3 percent do.

"I've never been denied opportunities because I'm gay," a lesbian pharmaceutical executive tells us. "In fact, I've had extra opportunities through the LGBTQ employee resource group here. It gave me the chance to build relationships and to be a leader early in my career."

Research affirms lesbians' relative advantage: a 2015 meta-analysis of thirty-one studies published between 1995 and 2012 shows lesbians worldwide earning a 9-percent wage premium over heterosexual women on average[40]—the so-called "lesbian premium." Another study suggests lesbians in the US enjoy a premium of 20 percent over heterosexual women.[41]

It is possible that not all of this salary premium is due to straight men getting along better (or believing that other straight men would get along better) with lesbian/bisexual women than with straight women. It may also have to do with career choices. "There's some evidence to suggest that lesbians go into jobs with more men in them—and the more men in the job, the higher the salary tends to be," Lee Badgett, an economics professor at the University of Massachusetts Amherst, said in an interview with the digital news outlet *Quartz*.[42]

It's worth noting that this "lesbian premium" exists only in comparison to straight women. A study indicates that lesbians still earn less on average than both gay and straight men.[43]

PART THREE
HOW BIAS DESTROYS
VALUE IN ORGANIZATIONS

10

Burning Out, Busting Out, and Blowing Up

As any professional who has experienced bias knows, its impact can be profound. Feeling misjudged by superiors damages productivity and commitment. It also represents a broader set of costs to the organization as a whole. One of the senior leaders whom we interviewed, Philippe Krakowsky of Interpublic Group Mediabrands, where he helped create the firm's diversity and inclusion strategy, cited bias's "huge" cost. "Whether we're missing out on great people's contributions or running the risk that they leave us, bias introduces gross inefficiencies," he says.

Another of the talent specialists who spoke with us, Karyn Twaronite, partner and global diversity and inclusiveness officer at EY, says, "If global companies want to remain competitive, they must create a bias-free zone in the workplace. How else can they possibly elicit and capture the ideas needed to reach the global marketplace?"

We found that employees who perceive ACE bias are more likely to engage in three costly activities: they burn out, bust out, or blow up. These represent significant costs to organizations through hits to employee engagement and retention and through an increased likelihood of employee sabotage.

BURNING OUT: NO LONGER EVEN TRYING

"Everyone knows that the ad industry is too white, that it doesn't reflect the country as a whole, and that's a problem for business," Monique, a young black account executive, says. "So here I am."

But even though her firm recruited her in part because of her background, now that she's at work, she's found that her insight into diverse markets is the last thing anyone wants. She describes meetings where her boss and clients casually discuss whether the chosen model for an advertising campaign is "European enough" or instead "too urban"—code for a person of color. When she speaks privately to her boss about ideas to convince clients to broaden their views of potential markets, and what kinds of campaigns might appeal to these markets, she just gets a frown in response.

When a wave of police violence against young black men made media headlines, her boss (a white woman from a wealthy family) casually announced to the whole office that she simply "couldn't understand" how anyone could be afraid of the police. Monique wanted to explain that her father and brother have both been harassed by police "for walking or driving while black." But she stayed quiet, fearful of playing to the "angry black woman" stereotype. "So much for trying to understand one giant part of this country," she says.

The constant need to edit herself also makes her feel increasingly alienated from her colleagues. "I'm the black sheep, literally," Monique says. "Most of my peers at the office are rich, white, former sorority girls whose parents supplement their paychecks so that they can afford to buy the latest fashions and go out to the city's hottest restaurant and clubs—my boss included. This is supposedly a fun place to work, but it's not for me. I do what I have to do to not get fired while I look for a way out."

Monique perceives bias in a number of categories, most notably connections: she feels that networks inside the company are closed to her and that the ones she has outside it are unvalued. Her ability to open up new markets is neglected. And she suspects that she's getting dinged on executive presence, since as a black woman, her boss probably considers her "too urban."

The disengagement and alienation that Monique exhibits as a result are common to those who suffer bias. Employees who perceive ACE bias are nearly three times as likely (20 percent vs. 7 percent) to say that they're disengaged at work. They are more than four times as likely (33 percent vs. 8 percent) to report that they feel regularly alienated at work. They are more than twice as likely (75 percent vs. 35 percent) to say, "I am not proud to work for my company." They're also 2.6 times as likely (34 percent vs. 13 percent) to have withheld ideas and market solutions over the previous six months.

The costs of alienated employees who are just going through the motions are immense. Gallup estimates that active disengagement costs the US $450 billion to $550 billion per year.[44]

Monique's company may also be taking a hit on market growth because of how her superiors are treating her. "I've got a whole set of different experiences, not just because I'm black, but because my parents are working class," she says. "I help them with their bills, not the other way around. I know what it's like to live paycheck to paycheck and be terrified that you won't make rent if you lose your job."

But even while Monique recognizes that her experience is business-relevant ("That's how a lot of the country lives, paycheck to paycheck: there's a gigantic market outside the elite bubble, and as an ad agency, we have to speak to them"), she keeps her insights to herself in an effort to downplay her differences. When her boss and colleagues talk about ski and beach vacations, she doesn't talk about going back home to a small Southern town to help her parents do the paperwork and taxes on their small business.

"If I could be myself a little more, I could contribute more to the company. I'm a natural relationship builder. I like people. But I'm always preoccupied about how I'm presenting myself here, and it's exhausting."

Employees who perceive ACE bias are 50 percent more likely than those who don't to expend some energy repressing parts of their persona at work (69 percent vs. 46 percent). When that happens, employers pay a price: employees who devote energy to hiding aspects of their identities are siphoning energy away from their jobs. Those who cannot bring their full selves to work are likewise denying their employers insight into markets and ideas with the power to unlock those markets.[45] In CTI's report *Innovation, Diversity, and Market Growth*, we found that when teams include even one member who represents the target consumer, the entire team is more than twice as likely to understand that consumer:[46]

TEAMS WHO UNDERSTAND THEIR TARGET CONSUMER BY CONSUMER DEMOGRAPHIC[47]

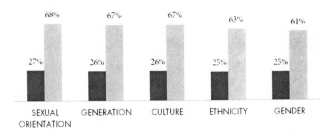

	SEXUAL ORIENTATION	GENERATION	CULTURE	ETHNICITY	GENDER
No team members match end user	27%	26%	26%	25%	25%
At least one team member matches end user	68%	67%	67%	63%	61%

But if such team members are suppressing their insights, it's logical to assume that this benefit is lost. Their teams are cut off from beneficial ideas about those end users.

Monique's company recruited her for added insights into the African-American market. Had her supervisors made her differences and experiences welcome, they also would have gained insight into working-class and rural America. Instead, they have an employee who is exhausted and bitter from the effort it takes to hide these experiences that could have been so valuable.

A COSTLY INVESTMENT, BUSTING OUT THE DOOR

Karina, a client relationship vice president at a global entertainment conglomerate, recently earned, with her employer's help, an MBA from one of the country's highest-rated business schools. But as soon as she's contractually permitted, she intends to take her new skills elsewhere.

It's every HR department's nightmare: invest in a high-potential employee only to see her depart, perhaps for a competitor. Direct replacement costs can reach as high as 50 to 60 percent of an employee's annual salary, with total costs associated with turnover ranging from 90 percent to 200 percent of an individual's annual salary.[48]

According to our data, nearly half (48 percent) of employees who perceive ACE bias have spent time at work looking for another job in the past six months. And the percentage of employees who report that they plan to leave their current companies within the year more than triples, to 31 percent from 10 percent, when they experience ACE bias.

Karina's current determination to leave would have been unthinkable for her a year ago when she thought that she was on a fast track to the top. Aside from the firm-sponsored MBA, her previous supervisor had indicated that she was grooming Karina to replace her as the North American department head. Yet when that particular supervisor left and her department was restructured, senior management confirmed suspicions that she'd long held.

"People who look like me just don't get put into senior positions here," Karina, who is Afro-Latina, says. "In all my time here, I haven't seen a single one." She reports that again and again she's seen a senior-level position open, then the standard selection process gets waived or modified to make room for a preferred candidate, who's always either white, male, or both.

With her, she says, the standard selection process was also modified—to her detriment.

When the position of North American head finally opened, she applied for it, but she was told that the rules had been changed. Senior management wanted to appoint a global head first. Months went by, a global head was appointed, and then the requirements changed again to include experience that Karina didn't have.

She decided to go out and get the new experience, then apply again. But before she even began her new rotation, the global head called her in and told her not to bother. "You probably won't get the position anyway," she said.

Like many of our interviewees, Karina says that for a long time she resisted attributing her difficulties to bias. "I wanted to believe that if I just worked harder and did even better, I'd get the job. But I've been killing my performance numbers. Nothing I do makes a difference."

Karina tells us that she could now try to switch divisions inside her company. Her previous supervisor was excellent. Perhaps her next one would be too. But she's decided it's not worth the bother. "The problem here is bigger than one person. I can't prove it's bias against people of color, but it sure feels like it. I want to rise a lot higher than I am now, and as soon as I can, I'm going someplace else to do it."

BLOWING UP: SABOTAGE

At the turn of the twenty-first century, Bridgestone/ Firestone Tires had to recall 14.4 million of its tires, some 6.5 million of which were on the road at the time. One in every four hundred tires experienced blowouts, putting all the company's customers at risk. The incident cost the company dearly in revenue—and in reputation.[49]

Yet some mystery surrounded this recall. Laboratory tests failed to identify any manufacturing or design flaw that could explain the surge in defective tires. If design and manufacturing were in good shape, what had caused this costly, dangerous problem?

The broadly accepted theory is that widespread employee error was to blame. But that answer leads to another question: why, after decades of reliable production, did workers suddenly start to make mistakes? A few facts point to a possible explanation: The tires were largely handmade and the workforce at the time was highly, publicly disgruntled. Not too long before the incident, Firestone had implemented mandatory twelve-hour shifts, seven-day-a-week operations, and lower hourly rates for new hires. When the workers went on strike, the company brought in temporary workers. After a year-long, bitter dispute, union workers got their jobs back, but their reentry into the workforce was contentious, to say the least. Factory conditions were called "brutal"—and at least one study has attributed the faulty products that came out of the Firestone factories during that time to severe workforce discontent.[50]

Firestone is an extreme example, but our data and interviews show that employees who perceive ACE bias lash out against their employers in ways large and small.

When employees perceive ACE bias, they are 4.5 times as likely to have intentionally failed to follow through on an important assignment in the past six months (9 percent to 2 percent).

Employees who perceive ACE bias are also more likely to damage the company's brand and harm recruitment.

Think of James Demore, a Google employee who published a ten-page memo about the company's diversity and inclusion efforts—and how he interpreted those efforts to exclude men. "Google has created several discriminatory practices," Demore wrote in his memo, including "programs, mentoring, and classes only for people with a certain gender or race." In other words, by being excluded from these programs, Demore felt his potential for building connections, executive presence, and other ACE model elements was being under-assessed by his employer. While Demore initially shared the ten-page memo broadly on an internal Google mailing list, it was soon leaked to the press and posted publicly in its entirety. Google responded by firing Demore.

Demore's decision to air his grievances so widely kicked off a series of events that have damaged Google's reputation as an employer—with those who agree with Demore's ideas, those who disagree with the company's decision to fire him, and those who see the company's atmosphere as chaotic or polarizing. Amid many reactions in the press, *New York Times* columnist David Brooks penned an op-ed headlined "Sundar Pichai Should Resign as Google's C.E.O."[51]; other headlines in the press ranged from "Behind the Google Diversity Memo Furor is Fear of Google's Vast, Opaque Power"[52] to "Diversity Training Was Supposed to Reduce Bias at Google. In Case of Fired Engineer, It Backfired."[53]

It's a tough reminder that bias truly is in the eye of the beholder—and that companies must remember that *any* employee who feels ACE bias, regardless of identity, wields the power to sabotage.

Carlos, whom we met in chapter eight, became an example after he perceived a double standard around ambition for Latinos. "I'd never badmouth the company, that would be unprofessional," he says. "But I've stopped posting positive things about it. When other people ask me about working there, I keep quiet or I change the subject. Everyone understands what my silence means, especially since I used to be so positive about this company."

Social media and word of mouth are key tools for companies to establish their brand among both consumers and potential employees. Every company would like to see its employees act as advocates for the organization in face-to-face and virtual networks.

Only 20 percent of employees who perceive ACE bias have ever referred someone to work at their companies, compared to 34 percent of those who don't perceive ACE bias. And with ACE bias, the odds that employees will speak and post negatively about their companies rises to 5 percent from 1 percent.

Five percent may not sound like a big number, but as we've shown, a single act of sabotage can go a long way.

Carlos notes how important word of mouth and social media reputation are for other companies as he considers where to go next. "There's a very strong community of Latino executives in my city. I listen to what they say, or don't say, about their companies and the culture there for people of color. If I hear of an opening in a firm with the right culture, I may try for it, even if the compensation is a little less than what I'm getting now. What I want is a place that will recognize my work and give me a fair chance to move up."

In the next Part, we'll look at some data-driven strategies to turn companies into organizations where everyone feels that they have a fair chance at success.

PART FOUR
SOLUTIONS

11

Strategies to Disrupt Bias

Bias, as both individual organizations and our society as a whole have discovered, is hard to disrupt. But our methodology handed us a way to connect with individuals who experience bias—and those who don't. Looking into the data, we could identify key conditions under which individuals are far less likely to experience bias. In this chapter, we'll lay out those conditions—and how you can create them at your company.

Here are the three conditions we find enormously impactful in cooling ACE bias:

- **Diversity in leadership** that breaks and expands leadership archetypes

- **Inclusive leaders** who elicit and listen to opinions from all

- **Sponsors** who level the playing field for advancement

In our work consulting with companies, we've discovered many systemic interventions to drive sponsorship, bring diversity to leadership, and build an inclusive leadership culture. None of these interventions require all managers to suddenly erase or perfectly compensate for their own unconscious biases. As blind auditions did for orchestra judges, these interventions aim to improve the corporate context, making it easier for supervisors and their reports to act without bias distorting their decisions and poisoning the air.

12

Diversify Leadership

It's not exactly headline news that corporate America's leadership doesn't adequately represent the diversity of the country's college-educated workforce or its domestic and global markets. But what our data shows is that diverse leadership can create an environment in which fewer employees experience bias.

We asked respondents, "Which kinds of diversity do you see in your company's leadership?" The options we offered were age, gender, race/ethnicity, religious background, socioeconomic background, sexual orientation, disability, and nationality. We defined the leadership of a respondent's company to be inherently diverse if it had at least three types of diversity represented.

Next, we made new heat maps, comparing employees in large companies with and without inherent diversity in leadership. For those without diverse leaders, the heat map darkens considerably (see following page).

Employees at large companies *with* diverse individuals in top jobs, meanwhile, are 64 percent less likely to perceive ACE bias (see page 87). In fact, while women

EMPLOYEES WITHOUT INHERENT DIVERSITY IN LEADERSHIP at large companies who perceive negative bias in their superiors' assessment of ACE elements

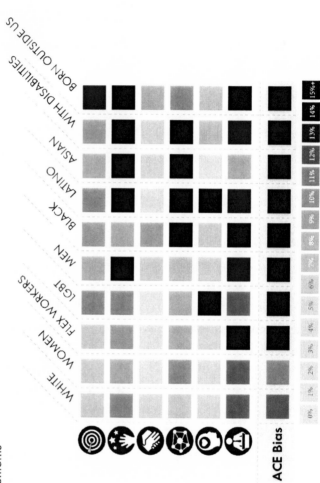

EMPLOYEES WITH INHERENT DIVERSITY IN LEADERSHIP at large companies who perceive negative bias in their superiors' assessment of ACE elements

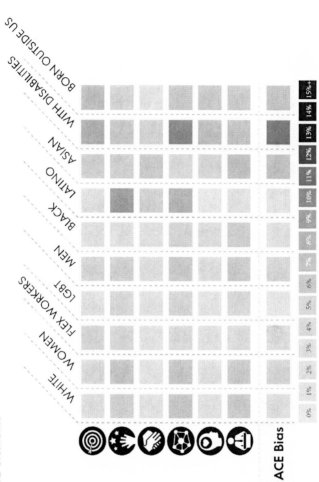

at organizations *without* diverse leadership are the least likely to perceive ACE bias (11.2 percent), they are still more likely to report ACE bias than women or any other group at companies *with* diverse leadership.

It's worth noting that when leadership is diverse, everyone's perception of bias declines—including whites, whose rate of reporting bias in two or more ACE elements drops more than 3.5 times, from 12.2 percent to 3.3 percent. Every talent cohort feels the benefits of diverse leadership.

How do diverse leaders help disrupt ACE bias? Part of the answer is the power of role models. Executives who are inherently diverse demonstrate by their presence that difference is valued and that diverse individuals can thrive at their organizations. They expand all employees' notions of who successful leaders are and undercut deep-seated biases. In a study that tested the efficacy of seventeen different bias interventions, the most effective proved to be a scenario that exposed participants to "counter-stereotypical exemplars" such as a malevolent white villain and a dashing black hero.[54]

Johnson & Johnson offers one example of how to boost diversity in management. The company has codified and socialized expectations of its leadership with its credo, which dates back to 1943. It cites, among other values, equal opportunity for employment, development, and advancement. Alongside other efforts to increase awareness of its credo, Johnson & Johnson has an annual survey to assess how well the company is living up to it, and an anonymous hotline employees can call to raise concerns about where the company may not be following its credo's standards. The credo sets the tone for both aspiration and accountability when it comes to bias and discrimination.

The credo influences decisions at Johnson & Johnson in many ways. When the company established its innovation centers in San Francisco, Boston, London, and China, it sought the best talent from all over the world regardless of gender, age, or ethnicity. Seema Kumar, vice president of innovation, global health, and policy communication, says the company makes inclusion—in all roles including leadership—a business priority because it greatly enhances overall organizational performance…and because it's the right thing to do.

But, she says, the talent pool of women and minorities for top leadership positions remains limited, in part attributable to decades of unconscious bias in the science fields in both industry and academia. Kumar is pleased that Johnson & Johnson is adopting a comprehensive, enterprise-wide approach to mitigating unconscious bias in the workplace through training and workshops, diversity mentorship programs, and programs that encourage girls to enter STEM disciplines and support women at every stage of their careers in the sciences.

Kumar is very pleased Johnson & Johnson recently appointed Ms. Rowan Chapman to lead its California innovation center. "Chapman represented both the best choice for the position and a strong champion for women in industry leadership positions," Kumar says. And, she added, "women in leadership roles have a long-term positive impact on eliminating unconscious bias. If a woman looks at the senior-most leadership and can't see herself among them one day, that will limit progress. But when women and minorities see people like themselves in top leadership roles, they recognize that they can succeed and the sky is the limit at Johnson & Johnson."

How can organizations build a leadership pipeline that disrupts bias by better reflecting the diversity of the talent pool? Such a pipeline is of course one of the goals of bias disruption, but to help start a virtuous cycle, our experience suggests four measures:

- **Hire and promote** candidates who embody and understand the power of difference.

- **Codify and socialize** company standards and expectations.

- **Implement a "tone from the top"** that endorses a variety of acceptable approaches to leadership.

- **Create role model videos and playbooks** of executives in action that feature diverse styles and approaches.

13

Hire, Train, and Evaluate for Inclusive Leadership

Inclusion is a common buzzword, but what does it mean when it comes to leadership? We addressed this question in our 2013 report *Innovation, Diversity, and Market Growth*. We were looking to see if there was a relationship between innovation and inclusion, and we concluded that inclusive leaders create a "speak-up culture" where team members feel welcome and included, feel free to share their ideas and opinions, and are confident their ideas will be heard and recognized. In other words, inclusive leaders solicit the kind of "collective genius" that Harvard Business School scholar Linda Hill has identified as crucial to an innovative company culture.[55] Our report found that leaders who exhibit at least three of these behaviors are more likely to achieve that culture:

- **Ensure all voices get heard**. That may mean making room for a remote team member or one whose first language isn't English to contribute, assigning every member a speaking role prior to the meeting, or silencing members who interrupt hesitant speakers or talk over quieter ones.

- **Make it safe to propose novel ideas**, such as by offering your own out-of-the-box ideas to show that radical notions carry no penalty.

- **Give actionable feedback.** Institutionalizing a five-minute debrief ("one thing you did well, one thing you need to work on") after every meeting is one possibility.

- **Take advice and implement feedback.** Don't just ask for input, but show that you're willing to change your mind as a result.

- **Empower decision-making among team members** by giving them ownership of pieces of your strategy and lending them the support they need to succeed.

- **Share credit for team success**, in part by cutting yourself out as the middleman and letting team members present directly to senior management.[56]

We asked respondents which of these behaviors their managers displayed. If their managers displayed at least three, we defined them as employees who have inclusive leaders. We then produced new heat maps for those who lack and those who have inclusive leaders (see pages 94 and 95).

When employees lack inclusive leaders, the heat map darkens.

But when employees have inclusive leaders, they're a stunning 87 percent less likely to perceive ACE bias, and 39 percent more likely to be engaged at work. Women's perception of ACE bias drops from 14.0 percent without inclusive leaders to 1.0 percent with such leaders. Latinos' perception of bias around their ambition drops from 19.2 percent without inclusive leaders to 3.8 percent with.

"My best manager, he laid it out clearly to everyone on his team what they had to do to get to the next level, and told us what we had to work on," an advertising executive in New York tells us. "That kind of feedback, along with the explicit criteria for getting ahead, made everyone feel they could do it if they tried."

"I had a great manager once," a healthcare marketing executive in Indianapolis says. "She said if we didn't have a chance to speak up during a meeting but had something to contribute, we should speak to her later or send an email. And she made it clear that she meant it. She occasionally would announce to the team that she'd received an email with a great idea from so-and-so. It made everyone eager to contribute, that they knew they'd be listened to."

Sometimes managers figure out on their own how to be inclusive. More often, their behavior is based on their own managers' attitudes. "At the company where

EMPLOYEES WITHOUT INCLUSIVE LEADERS at large companies who perceive negative bias in their superiors' assessment of ACE elements

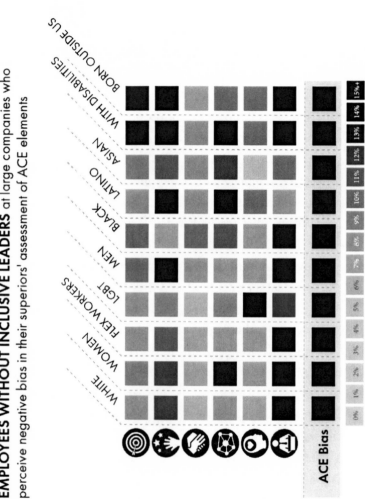

EMPLOYEES WITH INCLUSIVE LEADERS at large companies who perceive negative bias in their superiors' assessment of ACE elements

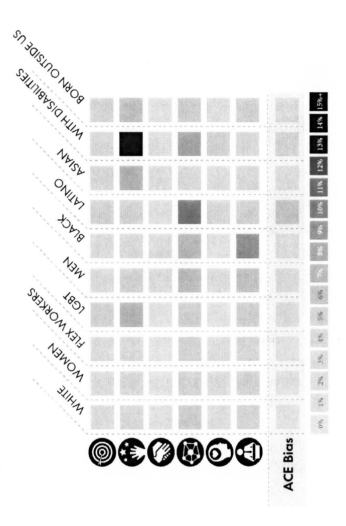

I started my career, managers were dinged if any of their reports didn't advance," a credit analyst at an asset manager in New York says. "Part of their rating came from how we were rated. Senior management's attitude was, 'We've hired these young people because they have a lot of potential. If they're not advancing, someone's not training them right.' So managers had incentives to tell us and support us if we weren't doing well."

"The inverse of bias is feeling welcomed, included, and valued for your difference," explains EY's Karyn Twaronite.

Among the many ways in which inclusive leadership makes a difference in bias, providing actionable feedback may be especially important. In prior CTI research, many women and people of color told us that they hardly ever received feedback, and when they did it was often too vague to be helpful (think of Tiffany in Chapter Six of this book.)[57]

A Harvard professor's recent study of cashiers in France may help explain why so many women and minorities complain that their leaders fail to give them constructive feedback. This study showed that biased managers (as measured by the IAT) interact far less with minority employees than they do with white ones, even if minority workers didn't report that these (rare) interactions were unpleasant or demonstrated hostility.[58]

Without interaction with management, unless there are strong formal procedures for feedback, employees may have a harder time learning about their weaknesses and improving them. Little wonder, then, that inclusive leaders have reports who are far less likely to perceive bias in how their potential is assessed. After all, inclusive leaders are adept at giving feedback and taking advice from all members of the team. It's not easy to be an inclusive leader, especially when you're leading people with whom you may not be fully comfortable. But it pays off.

When organizations succeed in encouraging inclusive leadership, everyone benefits. Latinos, for example, rather than feeling that their connections in their communities are not recognized, may be able to use these connections to boost their organizations' bottom lines.

Take Maribel Arias, senior vice president and executive field underwriter for Chubb, who observed that while the number of Latino-owned businesses was growing exponentially, the insurance industry wasn't taking notice. Using demographic data to make her case, she proposed to her manager an outreach strategy that drew on her own connections in the Latino community and face-to-face interactions with Latino managers. Thanks to her initiative, Chubb is today a vendor of choice for small- and medium-enterprise Latino business owners. "Having verbal support and encouragement from senior leadership, and having them put resources around an idea for a market that they themselves did not represent and did not necessarily understand, was proof that I can thrive here," she says.

How do we improve managers' communication habits and create a speak-up culture? Our experience and our Task Force members' advice offer these guidelines:

- Help top leaders set the tone through company town halls, where they can feature ideas from diverse employees and communicate that they believe in inclusive leadership and its value for driving innovation.

- Introduce managers to the six characteristics of inclusive leadership that encourage everyone to contribute ideas.

- Train managers and employees in dialogue skills to ensure that everyone gets heard.

- Build in accountability, preferably by linking managers' promotions and pay to exhibiting inclusive leader behaviors.

14

Support Diverse Talent with Sponsors

"To move up, it's so important for senior management to know who you are and know what you're doing long before the promotion decision is made," says Karina, whom we met in Part Three. "That's an area where a sponsor can make a big difference, but in my company you almost never see women or people of color having a sponsor." Not coincidentally, Karina, who is Afro-Latina, discourages acquaintances and friends from working at her company and is planning to leave as soon as she can.

Five CTI studies since 2010 suggest that Karina is right. We've studied sponsorship—or senior-level advocacy of high-potential talent—in many dimensions. Time and again, we find that diverse talent benefits from having sponsors to lever them into leadership. Such sponsors can effectively bypass or negate the effects of managerial bias. But top talent isn't sponsored equally in corporate America. Men are 46 percent more likely than women to have a sponsor,[59] and whites are 63 percent more likely than people of color to enjoy such advocacy.[60]

Sponsors, according to CTI research, are senior leaders who actively invest time and resources in their protégés, helping them access opportunities for career growth and advancement.[61] "The people in this firm who have sponsors, they hear about positions before they open, they learn what they have to do to get them, and they get a pass or permission to learn on the job if they lack experience," a black credit analyst told us. "But it's almost only white men who have those."

Like inclusive leaders, sponsors have a profoundly mitigating effect on the ACE bias that employees perceive. Sponsors see their protégés' potential clearly—and are willing to fight to make sure others see it, too. "I am where I am now because of a sponsor I had," says Sally, an Asian-American pharmaceutical executive. "I was promoted because she believed in me." Sally explains that she didn't "check every box that an HR computer might have generated" for her current position and that "just my résumé on someone's desk might not have gotten me the job." But Sally's sponsor knew her and her work and was willing to take a leap of faith for her. Sally is now sponsoring several people herself and hopes that she can one day help them rise up the ranks at the company. Not coincidentally, she praises her company and encourages people in her professional and social networks—Sally is a lesbian and Asian-American—to consider working there.

We reran our heat maps (see pages 102-103) to look for sponsorship's impact and found that employees with sponsors are 90 percent less likely to perceive ACE bias. They're also 21 percent more likely to be engaged at work.

Once again, the results cut across every talent cohort, including the most at-risk. With a sponsor, foreign-born talent's experience of bias in two or more ACE measures plunges from a threatening 16.2 percent to zero. Even for employees with disabilities, who remain most at risk, the perception of bias falls from 14.9 percent to 8.4 percent when they have sponsors.

What does successful sponsorship look like? It may look like what Danica Dilligard found when she arrived at Ernst & Young in 1997. Her appetite for hard work and yearning to move up in the world after a hardscrabble childhood reminded Mike Kacsmar of himself. But he also saw that hard work alone wouldn't carry her far. As a black woman from Panama, Dilligard was, by her own description, "a diamond in the rough," someone in need of support, guidance, and feedback. Kacsmar provided it. When Dilligard ruffled feathers in meetings, he coached her to tone down her style. "I didn't want to change who she was, I just wanted her to understand who was in her audience," he recalls. He helped her close skill gaps. When she stumbled with an important client, he worked with her to iron out the misunderstanding.

Most dramatically, Kacsmar worked relentlessly to shine a spotlight on Dilligard's growing achievements. He convinced a very senior female leader to "see what Dilligard brought to the table" and helped Dilligard gain

EMPLOYEES WITHOUT SPONSORS at large companies who perceive negative bias in their superiors' assessment of ACE elements

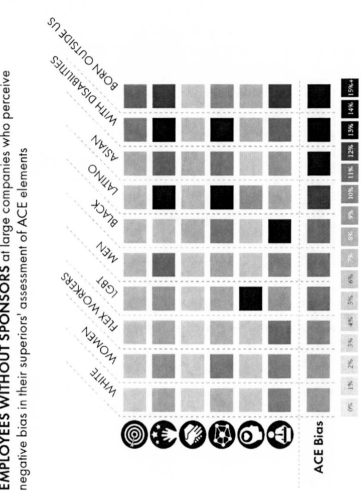

EMPLOYEES WITH SPONSORS at large companies who perceive negative bias in their superiors' assessment of ACE elements

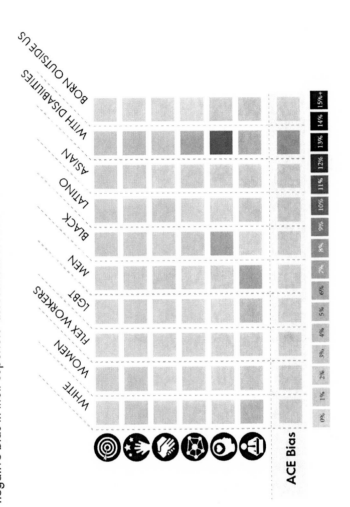

exposure to a range of senior leaders through strategic presentations and choice introductions. "In sessions where we talked about our best people, I would tell people that she was ready to be a partner," says Kacsmar. Dilligard, in turn, didn't let up on the gas pedal of her career—and never took Kacsmar's advocacy for granted. "I've benefited from the organic relationship we've built over the years, because I've put just as much into it," says Dilligard. "The stars aligned, in terms of meeting Mike, but also because of what I brought to the table."

How can companies have more employees who feel like Sally and Danica and fewer who feel like Karina? The key lies in systemic interventions that create (or reveal) incentives for those in power to make an effort to sponsor high-potential employees who may not look like them or have gone to the same schools as them.

"I sponsor a lot of people," Stephen Dunmore, chief executive officer of North America Schools at Sodexo, tells us. "They often don't know that I'm having impact on their careers by saying great things about them in a meeting. But I'm just one person. With a more formal sponsorship culture, we ensure the right people are actively sponsoring underrepresented talent so that they are getting fair representation in those meetings."

Many organizations have found success in leveling the playing field through initiatives that expose diverse talent to senior leaders over an extended period of time. The goal is for the extended exposure to make senior leaders more comfortable advocating for diverse talent.

At Booz Allen Hamilton, for example, diverse groups of high-potential employees spend months on teams tasked with solving business-critical problems identified by a market leader, then presenting their solutions at a capstone event attended by the senior leaders.[62] At Bank of America, men and women of color find sponsors through a program that ensures both parties understand their responsibilities in building a mutually beneficial nine-month strategic relationship.[63] Rather than create a stand-alone initiative, Deloitte embeds sponsorship into each of its existing leadership development programs.[64]

Intel's *Extending Our Reach*, a sponsorship program for women and people of color, has culminated in mobility for 40 percent of participants since its inception in 2011, with sixteen of them attaining vice-president-level promotions and one attaining the level of corporate vice president.[65] At another Fortune 100 financial services firm, 62 percent of participants in its women's sponsorship initiative have reported a change in their level of responsibility as a direct result of the program, with 69 percent reporting a new role and 46 percent reporting a new division.[66]

Ogilvy & Mather has prioritized inclusive sponsorship to diversify its leadership. "At Ogilvy, we are committed to creating a workforce as diverse as the clients that we work with and the brands that they represent," says Donna Pedro, senior partner and chief diversity officer. "As part of Global Chairman and CEO John Seifert's vision, we have created a pilot program to identify and sponsor thirty of our high-potential women in the USA. This program has led to more than half of our leadership positions today now being held by women, putting us well ahead of the industry."

We've found four measures that help an organization build a culture of sponsorship that is inclusive, rather than just another way to perpetuate the lack of diversity in leadership.

- **Educate and incentivize leaders.** Use hard data to demonstrate to leaders that sponsoring diverse talent isn't about altruism. It's about growing their companies' and their groups' bottom lines. Sponsoring diverse individuals provides built-in incentives—if managers know the data.

- **Educate rising stars on how to be stellar protégés.** Stress that sponsorship is not a gift; it must be earned. In past CTI research, we've discussed how individuals who consistently over-deliver, who are loyal to the organization and its mission, and who bring a distinctive "currency" (a complementary skill or network) can attract the investment of a sponsor.[67]

- **Create opportunities for diverse talent to show their leadership potential.** Help leaders see what diverse talent has to offer by making that talent more visible. Executives take notice of who's leading the firm's employee resource groups, who's driving philanthropic or volunteer endeavors, and even who's captaining the company sports teams. Steer diverse talent into those spotlights. Better yet, create high-visibility projects that get leaders and diverse talent working together toward a common goal.

- **Make leaders who sponsor diverse talent more visible**. Make it clear that the organization values their efforts, and create forums for them to evangelize to other leaders what they've gained from their investment.

15

A Playbook for Disrupting Bias

How can firms ensure their employees believe that their supervisors are giving them a fair chance to fulfill their ambitions? How can firms choose and deploy bias-busting interventions in the most cost-effective manner and maximize their contributions to the bottom line?

Based on the focus groups, interviews, nationally representative survey, and external research synthesized in this book, we offer a playbook for adding value through mapping bias, understanding where it imposes the most costs on an organization, and disrupting it at those pain points.

STEP ONE: DO YOUR OWN DIAGNOSTIC

- **Field a survey** among your employees to determine whether and how they perceive bias. Focus your questions on assessments of different elements of leadership potential—since assessments of potential shape employees' futures—rather than on their past progress up the management ladder. We recommend that you use whatever criteria your organization has to assess potential in employees. The ACE measures—ability, ambition, connections, commitment, emotional intelligence, and executive presence—can also serve as a guide. On each aspect of potential, the key questions are how you assess yourself, how you think your superiors assess you, and what kind of feedback you have received. Employees' opinions of their supervisors' judgments should be based on concrete feedback if available, and on a general impression if not.

- **Sort respondents** within each aspect of potential into:

  - Those who report that their supervisors rate them equal or better than their self-assessment; these employees do not perceive negative bias

  a. Those who report that their supervisors are giving them assessments worse than they give themselves; these respondents perceive negative bias.

STEP TWO: INTERPRET THE DIAGNOSTIC

- **Examine talent cohorts** of interest to your organization (e.g., foreign nationals, blacks, veterans) to learn which are most likely to perceive bias. Different organizations will have different talent cohorts at different levels of risk.

- **Conduct an inquiry** to get the context for counterintuitive findings. Anonymous, web-based focus groups such as CTI's Insights In-Depth® sessions are one highly effective method of eliciting insights from employees who've reported bias in order to confirm and understand survey results.

- **Apply filters** to test whether employees with sponsors, employees with inclusive team leaders, or employees with diverse leaders in their business units or divisions are least likely to experience ACE bias in your corporate context. The answer will help you determine which of the three interventions you should prioritize. If your sample size is large enough, sort these results according to your most at-risk talent cohorts. (For example, if Latinos are most likely to perceive bias within your organization, look at which intervention makes Latinos least likely to report bias.)

STEP THREE: DISRUPT BIAS

Use the three bias-busting interventions, but not necessarily in the order that follows. Instead, prioritize the roll-out of these interventions based on your survey findings of the cohorts with the deepest needs and the most effective approaches to support them.

1. **Expand leadership archetypes**

   - Hire and promote candidates who embody difference.

   - Codify and socialize company standards and expectations.

   - Implement a "tone from the top" that endorses a variety of acceptable approaches to leadership.

   - Create role model videos and playbooks of executives in action, featuring a diversity of leadership styles and backgrounds.

2. **Train managers to be inclusive leaders**

   - Have top leaders set the tone through town halls, where they can feature ideas from diverse employees and communicate that they believe in inclusive leadership and its value for driving innovation.

   - Introduce managers to the six behaviors that prompt everyone to contribute ideas and communicate openly with their managers and colleagues.

   - Ensure everyone gets heard: train managers in dialogue skills.

   - Build accountability and incentives into annual performance reviews on the six inclusive leader behaviors.

3. **Build a culture of inclusive sponsorship**

    - Educate and incentivize leaders.

    - Educate rising stars on how to be stellar protégés.

    - Create opportunities for diverse talent to show their leadership potential.

    - Make leaders who sponsor diverse talent more visible.

STEP FOUR: RE-FIELD THE DIAGNOSTIC

After giving time for your interventions to have an effect, see where you've succeeded in reducing the perception of bias and see where bias lingers. Based on your updated survey data, disrupt again.

16

Best Bias-Busting Practices

In the course of our research, we discovered many companies who are experimenting with exciting programs and campaigns to build awareness of bias and start to root it out in systems and processes. We share the case studies here, so that you might learn from what others are doing and experiment with similar approaches within your own walls.

Something to keep in mind: Many companies employ a traditional 9-box evaluation model for assessments of performance and potential during annual employee reviews. The 9-box consists of a three-by-three matrix; on one axis is "performance," and on the other, "potential." The 9-box reduces employees to a single number: someone who has high potential and high performance will be a 9 (the box in the top right corner of the matrix), while someone who has low potential and low performance will be a 1 (the box in the bottom left corner of the matrix). In this chapter, we will explore how companies intent on disrupting bias are creatively supplementing the 9-box model—or in some cases, replacing it altogether.

SHEDDING LIGHT ON BIAS

Bloomberg—Parent Transition Coaching Program

Bloomberg designed and launched a Parent Experience Enhancement program to help employees navigate work/life challenges, address potential bias against employees taking parental leave, and help managers be as supportive as possible.

The program includes workshops and coaching for employees who take parental leave, as well as training for managers. The group workshops help parents support one another, building community and sharing stories, as they prepare for leave and return from it. In addition to group sessions, parents are able to participate in action-oriented one-on-one coaching with an external coach.

The program also helps managers support team members with new parenting responsibilities. Bloomberg offers quarterly workshops for managers of parents who are taking primary or secondary caregiver leave. "Bias may arise if other team members see coworkers coming in late or leaving early. It leaves them wondering, 'What about me?'" explains Drew Gulley, a program manager of diversity and inclusion at Bloomberg. "It's critical to have managers address the arrangement terms with their whole teams so that no one feels like they're being left out. Parents should receive due credit if they're coming in hours earlier than everyone else, or if they're accomplishing work from home."

While the program is still in its pilot phase across the United States and the United Kingdom, Gulley is confident, based on feedback thus far, that the program will make a measurable difference at scale. "Being a parent can be a nonapparent dimension of diversity in the workplace, one that's not always acknowledged," he points out. "Parents are keenly aware of this—and they value the fact that Bloomberg is putting resources into combatting possible parental bias."

Johnson & Johnson – Unconscious Bias Workshops

Johnson & Johnson held workshops on unconscious bias conducted by Professor Mahzarin R. Banaji, a distinguished scholar on the subject, to educate leaders on the nature of unconscious bias. In the first year, 33 percent of Johnson & Johnson's thirty-thousand-person population of managers and above took part in the three-hour workshops, with the goal of full participation over the next two years. The feedback has been overwhelmingly positive, with 91 percent of participants saying they feel they can apply what they've learned in Professor Banaji's workshops directly to their jobs.

The concepts of unconscious bias and inclusive leadership are being embedded into all programs and training that Johnson & Johnson provides to people leaders at multiple levels. "We hope to reach these leaders at key moments in their development and careers and arm them with the appropriate understanding and capabilities to be inclusive leaders. We know this is key to advancing a culture of belonging for everyone at Johnson & Johnson," explains Chief Diversity and Inclusion Officer Wanda Bryant Hope.

RETHINKING TALENT ASSESSMENT FRAMEWORKS

Deutsche Bank—Talent Indicators

To better understand employees' concerns about the company's talent review system, Deutsche Bank undertook an analysis of 1,500 interviews, several surveys, business data information, regulatory feedback, and employee anecdotal feedback. It became clear that measuring employees solely on performance and potential left too much room for often unintentional bias and failed to serve Deutsche Bank's talent fairly. Hence, Deutsche Bank endeavored to create something new that wouldn't be systematically biased by gender, age, or tenure.

Deutsche Bank decided to retire the traditional 9-box grid working on potential and performance only and introduced the total performance indicators. Initially, the indicators consisted of only three measures: capability, capacity for improvement, and future recommendation (i.e., whether the employee should advance, move into a new position at the same rank, or not move roles at all). "To reduce subjectivity, we ask a series of questions instead of asking for a rating," explains Global Head for Performance, Engagement, and Culture Birthe

Mester. Indeed, managers only have three options for each measure; for example, on the "capability" measure, the options are "has more capabilities than needed for current role," "capabilities are well-matched," or "has some but not all capabilities required." These measurements allow HR to get a more accurate picture of why an employee might not be advancing, and to address discrepancies with their managers. For example, if a manager says someone "has more capabilities than needed" but also gives a future recommendation that the individual should "not move," HR can follow up with that manager to ask why someone so capable shouldn't advance.

After continuously positive feedback, Deutsche Bank has added more dimensions of potential to employee assessments. These include contribution, business delivery and behavior, and individual experience (i.e., how long the employee has been in the organization and the time since their last promotion). In bringing all this information together for the first time in one synthesized evaluation, Mester sees Deutsche Bank's talent evaluation practices transforming from a numerical rating system into a tool that actually fosters employee development. "It is changing the way we assess and reflect on our people's talent," she explains. "People don't want to be reduced to a single rating. If we make the data transparent, they can have a real and productive conversation with their manager about their future at Deutsche Bank."

EY—Preference, Tradition, or Requirement?

Ernst & Young LLP's (EY) Preference Tradition Requirement (PTR) decision-making framework has become a central component of the professional services organization's strategy for combating bias. The premise is simple: when looking at someone's fit for a job or assignment, for example, reviewers consider whether any concerns about the candidate reflect a manager's personal preference, an organizational tradition, or a concrete job requirement. PTR can be leveraged in talent processes occurring organization-wide, whether they involve recruitment, promotion, team dynamics, or the way work is assigned and to whom.

"Is this a preference of my own? Is it an established tradition? Or is it really absolutely necessary to get the job done—a requirement?" explains Yvonne Breitenfeld, an associate director supporting diversity and inclusiveness at EY. The PTR framework facilitates equitable recruiting and promotional practices and offers a courteous way to challenge biased criticisms of employees and candidates. For example, if someone comments during a review that the individual "gets her work done efficiently but is not in the office five days a week," PTR empowers colleagues to speak up in a nonthreatening way and ask, "What I'm hearing you say is this person is performing and contributing in a meaningful way, but it's your preference that this person is in the office? Or is it a tradition? Is it truly a requirement?"

The "tradition" aspect of PTR provides an avenue to question any company norms that might be marginalizing the talent most vulnerable to bias. "This has been embraced by many of our business units," describes Breitenfeld. "It's become a language that we are using to help our people disrupt these conversations and take that pause, to really think through their decisions and judgments and the intentions behind them."

LEVELING THE PLAYING FIELD

BP—Rules of the Road

To help increase the number of women in senior roles and ensure parity in its recruitment policies, BP developed "Rules of the Road" principles for recruitment and selection to help managers address the systemic gender biases at play in promotion decisions. "When it's time to fill a senior role, we often hear that there are no qualified women available," explains Andrew Ditty, who until recently was head of Downstream HR at BP, identifying one of the organization's greatest challenges in ensuring fair internal succession plans.

The solution? Requiring that hiring managers include a suitably qualified woman on the shortlist to fill any senior-level position. If such a candidate is not available internally, leaders are expected to look more broadly in the organization and to look externally. And, if a woman ultimately isn't chosen for the role, the selection panel—which should also include a woman— must explain why and consider actions to ensure woman candidates are available for similar roles in the future. In the five years since the rule's adoption within BP's Downstream business, women's representation in BP's Downstream senior ranks has grown from 15 percent to 23 percent—an increase of just over 50 percent. Rather than allow selection panels to "opt in" to hiring female talent, the "Rules of the Road" force them to justify "opting out." Ditty is confident that, at this rate, BP will continue to make significant progress, increasing female representation in its senior ranks by 2020. Moving forward, BP seeks to employ this strategy on a wider scale, addressing other diverse groups as well as job openings at more junior levels. "We're looking at the whole pipeline, at all levels," explains Ditty. "We're trying to be conscious, inclusive, and sustainable. It's taken a lot of effort to do this in a merit-based way, but we've made sure we're filling and replenishing the pipeline with really strong talent—women and men."

Johnson & Johnson—Manager Reminders

At Johnson & Johnson, reminders and suggestions help to mitigate unconscious bias in performance evaluations. During the performance and development process, tips and suggestions are provided to managers on unconscious bias and how it may impact their thinking. These "nudges" provide a framework for managers that helps to enhance the objectiveness and productiveness of development conversations. "By embedding these practical 'just-in-time' reminders within our performance and development approach, we further ensure that diversity and inclusion is not an add-on but rather an integral part of our talent evaluation process," explains Wanda Bryant Hope, chief diversity and inclusion officer.

CHANGING THE CONVERSATION ABOUT BIAS

IPG—Vectors Model

IPG's IDEAL program (Interpublic Diverse Emerging and Aspiring Leadership) is a leadership development program that supports the advancement of high-potential diverse talent—and, as part of its strategy, includes proactive steps to minimize bias's impact on that advancement. One feature of the program to minimize bias is a transparent discussion between managers and their direct reports about career aspirations and development needs that results in plans based on specific criteria and measurable milestones.

IDEAL also seeks to mitigate bias by helping both participants and managers understand and discuss how bias can affect their careers without putting managers on the defensive. The program gives participants a model, called Vectors, to understand and address implicit bias without accusing one another of explicit bias. The Vectors model, created by Terrence Simmons at KornFerry Hay, posits that, in every workplace, invisible forces lead to privilege or disadvantage. These forces, headwinds and tailwinds, called "Vectors," include cultural norms, assumptions or stereotypes, and organizational traditions.

The IDEAL program trains the participants and their managers to address individual and institutional bias in a nonthreatening way using the Vectors model and language. They learn how to pinpoint the Vectors at play, to describe them and provide examples, and to have effective dialogues using neutral, constructive language. In addition, they can take the language back to their teams, and are encouraged to proactively identify the perceived Vectors at play in their environments.

For example, a new high-potential employee who is most productive when working remotely could encounter conflict with a manager who identifies strongly with an organizational tradition of doing all work in the office and attending all meetings in person. Establishing a common language—in this case, the Vector "power of organizational tradition"—to frame such conflict allows both managers and high-potentials to have the necessary conversations and address such differences.

These Vectors conversations, and the IDEAL program as a whole, are the first step toward bridging these divides, says Heide Gardner, chief diversity and inclusion officer at IPG. "You can't necessarily implement the same program across the organization," Gardner explains, "but you can influence others by imparting awareness and skill sets to high-potential talent." The results of this training speak for themselves: IPG has seen a 61-percent promotion rate for the initial group of IDEAL participants, and of the fifty managers and fifty employees who have gone through the program, 100 percent state that they plan to use the Vectors model in their jobs on a day to day basis.

Ogilvy & Mather—Courageous Conversations

In an effort to encourage "courageous conversations" around gender bias, Ogilvy & Mather holds Gender Dialogues workshops in all offices across the USA, led by Ogilvy & Mather's senior leadership teams. Over the course of two weeks, participants join workshops on self-awareness, building skills, and taking action. Fully 75 percent of employees in the New York office have taken part—along with 100 percent of employees in both the Atlanta and Washington, DC offices.

Donna Pedro, chief diversity officer, says habits transform once participation rates reach critical mass and employees feel compelled to speak up. "In most cases, someone isn't intending to put a woman leader down or not invite her out with the boys," she explains. "Things happen organically, and if you don't point them out, they're going to keep happening."

Gender Dialogues 2.0 will focus more on skill-building to initiate and engage in these conversations as productively as possible. As a starting point, a simple "SBI" framework—situation, behavior, impact—teaches participants to start these conversations by first acknowledging the situation at hand, then identifying the colleague's biased behavior, and finally explaining how that behavior impacts themselves or others. "The goal is for everyone in every office to speak that common language," says Pedro. "Then, we have universal preparedness to address unconscious bias in the moments it matters most.

Cardinal Health—Role Modeling and Blind Spots

How you say something is just as important as what you say. This language distinction is particularly important when it comes to matters of inclusion, especially biases. Cardinal Health has made some positive steps forward in this journey. By acknowledging "blind spots" rather than using the negatively charged word "bias," employees feel more comfortable admitting to the shortcomings in their own understanding and experiences. Senior leaders at Cardinal Health strengthen this willingness to be vulnerable by talking openly and visibly about their own blind spots.

Chief Financial Officer Mike Kaufmann makes a point of acknowledging his own vulnerabilities, saying, "It's okay to say 'I don't know' when you're presented with a situation of uncertainty." This openness has a "trickle-down" effect on other employees, explains Lisa Gutierrez, vice president of diversity and inclusion at Cardinal Health. "Because of role models like Mike, our leaders are having their own 'moments of truth' in decision making around their behaviors and how they view talent—especially talent that doesn't look or sound like them. These realizations result in more inclusive conversations."

Gutierrez feels the organization is moving in the right direction by speaking about bias in this way. "Traditionally, getting someone to acknowledge and act on their own biases can trigger feelings of shame or blame. It's hard to guarantee positive outcomes once this happens," she explains. "Acknowledging our blind spots at a personal and a leadership level, on the other hand, takes courage. We've found that many Cardinal Health leaders are willing to serve as active champions to others in the organization."

One leader, who has been with Cardinal Health almost three decades, found his blind spot with the LGBTQ community during a leadership session. As a straight white man and a respected leader, he realized his silence on issues implied indifference or reluctant consent. "I see clearly that I could have been a force for change, but I wasn't. This bothers me greatly. I am glad that I can do something about it going forward." he told Gutierrez. He now uses his position of power as a senior leader to acknowledge his blind spots openly and become an advocate for other allies.

ENDNOTES

1. Claudia Goldin and Cecilia Rouse, "Orchestrating Impartiality: The Impact of 'Blind' Auditions on Female Musicians," *NBER Working Paper Series*, January 1997: doi:10.3386/w5903.

2. Ibid.

3. See for example: Yassmin Abdel-Magied, "What Does My Headscarf Mean to You?" filmed December 2014, TED video, 14:01, https://www.ted.com/talks/yassmin_abdel_magied _what_does_my_headscarf_mean_to_you; Mahzarin R. Banaji and Anthony G. Greenwald, *Blindspot: Hidden Biases of Good People* (New York: Delacorte Press, 2013); Malcolm Gladwell, *Blink: The Power of Thinking Without Thinking* (New York: Little, Brown and Co., 2005).

4. See for example: Mahzarin R. Banaji and Anthony G. Greenwald, *Blindspot: Hidden Biases of Good People* (New York: Delacorte Press, 2013); Howard J. Ross, *Everyday Bias: Identifying and Navigating Unconscious Judgments in Our Daily Lives* (London: Rowman & Littlefield, 2016).

5. For data collected and referenced in this book, "Latino" refers to those who identify as "Latino" or "Hispanic."

6. Mitra Toossi, "A Look at the Future of the US Labor Force to 2060," Office of Occupational Statistics and Employment Projections, Bureau of Labor Statistics, September 2016, https://www.bls.gov/spotlight/2016/a-look-at-the-future-of -the-us-labor-force-to-2060/home.htm.

7. Sylvia Ann Hewlett, Melinda Marshall, and Laura Sherbin, with Tara Gonsalves, *Innovation, Diversity, and Market Growth* (New York: Center for Talent Innovation, 2013), 51-52.

8. Anthony G. Greenwald and Mahzarin R. Banaji, "Implicit Social Cognition: Attitudes, Self-Esteem, and Stereotypes," *Psychological Review* 102, no. 1 (1995): 4-27, https://faculty .washington.edu/agg/pdf/Greenwald_Banaji_PsychRev_1995 .OCR.pdf.

9. Kaiyuan Xu, Brian Nosek, and Anthony G. Greenwald, "Psychology Data from the Race Implicit Association Test on the

Project Implicit Demo Website," *Journal of Open Psychology Data* 2, no. 1 (2014): e3, http://doi.org/10.5334/jopd.ac.

10. Mahzarin Banaji and Anthony Greenwald, *Blindspot: Hidden Biases of Good People* (New York: Delacourt Press, 2013), 46-51.

11. Xu, Nosek, and Greenwald, "Race IAT" (see note 9).

12. Mary P. Rowe, "Barriers to Equality: The Power of Subtle Discrimination to Maintain Unequal Opportunity," *Employee Responsibilities and Rights Journal* 3, no. 2 (1990): 153-63, http://citeseerx.ist.psu.edu/viewdoc/download ?doi=10.1.1.370.2606&rep=rep1&type=pdf.

13. Ellen Huet, "Rise of the Bias Busters: How Unconscious Bias Became Silicon Valley's Newest Target," *Forbes*, November 2, 2015, https://www.forbes.com/sites/ellenhuet/2015/11/02/ rise-of-the-bias-busters-how-unconscious-bias-became-silicon -valleys-newest-target/#2818425819b5.

14. Sheryl Sandberg, "Managing Unconscious Bias," Facebook Newsroom, July 28, 2015, https://newsroom.fb.com/ news/2015/07/managing-unconscious-bias/; "You Don't Know What You Don't Know: How Our Unconscious Minds Undermine the Workplace," Google Blog, September 25, 2015, https://googleblog.blogspot.com/2014/09/you-dont-know -what-you-dont-know-how.html.

15. Capital One is one such example of a company cascading its bias training from senior to middle management; see "Focusing on the Future, Together," Capital One, accessed April 25, 2017, https://www.capitalone.com/inclusion/inspiring-tomorrow.

16. Joann S. Lublin, "Bringing Hidden Biases into the Light: Big Businesses Teach Staffers How 'Unconscious Bias' Impacts Decisions," *The Wall Street Journal*, January 9, 2014, https://www.wsj.com/articles/bringing-hidden-biases-into -the-light-1389311814?tesla=y.

17. Elizabeth Levy Paluck and Donald P. Green, "Prejudice Reduction: What Works? A Review and Assessment of Research and Practice," *Annual Review of Psychology* 60 (2009): 339-67.

18. Jesse Singal, "Psychology's Favorite Tool for Measuring Racism Isn't Up to the Job," *New York Magazine*, January 11, 2017, http://nymag.com/scienceofus/2017/01/psychologys-racism -measuring-tool-isnt-up-to-the-job.html.

19. Daniel Kahneman, *Thinking, Fast and Slow* (New York: Farrar, Straus and Giroux, 2011).

20. Alexandra Kalev, Frank Dobbin, and Erin Kelly, "Best Practices or Best Guesses? Assessing the Efficacy of Corporate Affirmative Action and Diversity Policies," *American Sociological Review* 71 (August 2006): 604, https://www.cfa.harvard.edu/cfawis /Dobbin_best_practices.pdf.

21. Ibid.

22. Frank Dobbin and Alexandra Kalev, "Why Diversity Programs Fail," *Harvard Business Review*, July/August 2016, https://hbr .org/2016/07/why-diversity-programs-fail.

23. United States Department of Education, "Bachelor's, Master's, and Doctor's Degrees Conferred by Postsecondary Institutions, by Sex of Student and Discipline Division: 2013-14," Institute of Education Sciences, National Center for Education Statistics, accessed April 26, 2017, https://nces.ed.gov/programs/digest /d15/tables/dt15_318.30.asp?current=yes; United States Department of Education, "Bachelor's Degrees Conferred by Postsecondary Institutions, by Race/Ethnicity and Sex of Student: Selected Years, 1976-77 through 2014-15," Institute of Education Sciences, National Center for Education Statistics, accessed April 26, 2017, https://nces.ed.gov/programs/digest /d16/tables/dt16_322.20.asp?current=yes; United States Department of Education, "Master's Degrees Conferred by Postsecondary Institutions, by Race/Ethnicity and Sex of Student: Selected Years, 1976-77 through 2014-15," Institute of Education Sciences, National Center for Education Statistics, accessed April 26, 2017, https://nces.ed.gov/programs/digest /d16/tables/dt16_323.20.asp?current=yes; United States Department of Education, "Doctor's Degrees Conferred by Postsecondary Institutions, by Race/Ethnicity and Sex of Student: Selected Years, 1976-77 through 2014-15," Institute of Education Sciences, National Center for Education Statistics, accessed April 26, 2017, https://nces.ed.gov/programs/digest /d16/tables/dt16_324.20.asp?current=yes; Equal Employment Opportunity Commission, "2015 Job Patterns for Minorities and Women in Private Industry (EEO-1)," US Equal Employment Opportunity Commission, accessed April 25, 2017, https://www1.eeoc.gov/eeoc/statistics/employment/jobpat -eeo1/2015/index.cfm#select_label; Valentina Zarya, "Female Fortune 500 CEOs Are Poised to Break This Record in 2017,"

Fortune, December 22, 2016, http://fortune.com/2016/12/22
/female-fortune-500-ceos-2017/; "Black Fortune 500 CEOs
Decline by 33%," Diversity Inc., June 30, 2015,
http://bestpractices.diversityinc.com/talent-management
/shortfalls-and-bias-driven-discrepancies-war-for-talent/black
-fortune-500-ceos-decline-by-33-in-past-year/.

24. Singal, "Psychology's Favorite Tool" (see note 18).

25. A. Colella and D.L. Stone, "Workplace Discrimination toward
Persons with Disabilities: A Call for Some New Research
Directions," in *Discrimination at Work: The Psychological and
Organizational Bases*, ed. R. Dipboye and A. Colella (Mawhah,
NJ: Erlbaum, 2005), 227-53.

26. Noni Allwood and Laura Sherbin, *Latinos at Work: Unleashing
the Power of Culture* (New York: Center for Talent Innovation,
2016), 16-18.

27. "People: Adriana Ocampo: Science Program Manager, NASA,"
National Aeronautics and Space Administration, accessed May
16, 2017, https://solarsystem.nasa.gov/people/ocampoa.

28. William Petersen, "Success Story, Japanese-American Style,"
The New York Times Magazine, January 9, 1966.

29. Jeff Guo, "The Staggering Difference between Rich Asian
Americans and Poor Asian Americans," *Washington Post*,
December 20, 2016, https://www.washingtonpost.com/news
/wonk/wp/2016/12/20/why-asian-americans-arent-as-rich-as
-they-seem.

30. Kenji Kuramitsu, "The Model Minority Myth and the Wedge
Between Black and White America," *Inheritance*, April 4, 2017,
https://inheritancemag.com/article/the-model-minority-myth
-and-the-wedge-between-black-and-white-america.

31. Liza Mundy, "Cracking the Bamboo Ceiling," *The Atlantic*,
November 2014, https://www.theatlantic.com/magazine
/archive/2014/11/cracking-the-bamboo-ceiling/380800/.

32. Qin Zhang, "Asian Americans beyond the Model Minority
Stereotype: The Nerdy and the Left Out," *Journal of
International and Intercultural Communication* 3, no.1 (2010):
20-37, doi:10.1080/17513050903428109.

33. Sylvia Ann Hewlett and Tai Green, *Black Women: Ready to Lead*
(New York: Center for Talent Innovation, 2015).

34. Anissa I. Vines et al., "Social Correlates of the Chronic Stress of Perceived Racism among Black Women," *Ethnicity & Disease* 16, no. 1 (2006): 101-7, https://www.ncbi.nlm.nih.gov/pmc/articles/PMC2865131/.

35. Hewlett and Green, *Black Women* (see note 33).

36. Ibid.

37. Ibid.

38. "Neuroscientists Find Evidence for 'Visual Stereotyping,'" New York University [Press Release], May 2, 2016, http://www.nyu.edu/about/news-publications/news/2016/may/neuroscientists-find-evidence-for-visual-stereotyping.html.

39. Allwood and Sherbin, *Latinos at Work* (see note 26).

40. Marieka Klawitter, "Meta-Analysis of the Effects of Sexual Orientation on Earnings," *Industrial Relations* 54, no.1 (January 2015): 4-32, http://onlinelibrary.wiley.com/doi/10.1111/irel.12075/abstract.

41. Nick Drydakis, "Sexual Orientation and Labor Market Outcomes," IZA World of Labor, December 2014, 4, https://wol.iza.org/uploads/articles/111/pdfs/sexual-orientation-and-labor-market-outcomes.pdf.

42. Neha Thirani Bagri, "New Research Confirms the 'Sexuality Pay Gap' is Real," *Quartz*, January 12, 2017, https://qz.com/881303/eight-million-americans-are-affected-by-a-pay-gap-that-no-one-talks-about/.

43. M.V. Lee Badgett et al., "Bias in the Workplace: Consistent Evidence of Sexual Orientation and Gender Identity Discrimination 1998-2008," *Chicago-Kent Law Review* 84, no.2 (2009): 559-95, http://scholarship.kentlaw.iit.edu/cklawreview/vol84/iss2/7/.

44. Gallup, "State of the American Workplace: Employee Engagement Insights for US Business Leaders," Gallup Inc., September 22, 2014, http://www.gallup.com/services/176708/state-american-workplace.aspx.

45. Kenji Yoshino, Sylvia Ann Hewett, *Out in the World: Securing LGBT Rights in the Global Marketplace* (New York: Center for Talent Innovation, 2016).

46. Hewlett et al., *Innovation* (see note 7).

47. Ibid.

48. David G. Allen, "Retaining Talent: A Guide to Analyzing and Managing Employee Turnover," SHRM Foundation, 2008, https://www.shrm.org/hr-today/trends-and-forecasting /special-reports-and-expert-views/Documents/Retaining-Talent .pdf.

49. Alan B. Krueger and Alexandre Mas, "Strikes, Scabs, and Tread Separations: Labor Strife and the Production of Defective Bridgestone/Firestone Tires," *The Journal of Political Economy* 112, no. 2 (April 2004): 253-89, doi:10.1086/381479.

50. Ibid.

51. David Brooks, "Sundar Pichai Should Resign as Google's C.E.O.," *New York Times*, August 11, 2017, https://www.nytimes.com /2017/08/11/opinion/sundar-pichai-google-memo-diversity .html.

52. Ezra Klein, "Behind the Google Diversity Memo Furor is Fear of Google's Vast, Opaque Power," *Vox*, August 10, 2017, https://www.vox.com/new-money/2017/8/10/16119338 /google-diversity-memo-damore-gender-sexist.

53. David Pierson and Tracey Lien, "Diversity Training Was Supposed To Reduce Bias at Google. In Case of Fired Engineer, It Backfired," *Los Angeles Times*, August 9, 2017, http://www .latimes.com/business/technology/la-fi-tn-james-damore -google-20170809-story.html.

54. Calvin K. Lai et al., "Reducing Implicit Racial Preferences: I. A Comparative Investigation of 17 Interventions," *Journal of Experimental Psychology* 143, no. 4 (August 2014): 1765, doi:10.1037/a0036260.

55. Linda A. Hill, Greg Brandeau, Emily Truelove, and Kent Lineback, *Collective Genius: The Art and Practice of Leading Innovation* (Cambridge: Harvard Business Review, 2014).

56. Hewlett et al., *Innovation* (see note 7).

57. Sylvia Ann Hewlett, Maggie Jackson, and Ellis Cose, with Courtney Emerson, *Vaulting the Color Bar: How Sponsorship Levers Multicultural Professionals into Leadership* (New York: Center for Talent Innovation, 2012); Sylvia Ann Hewlett, Noni Allwood, Karen Sumberg, and Sandra Scharf, with Christina Fargnoli, *Cracking the Code: Executive Presence*

and Multicultural Professionals (New York: Center for Talent Innovation, 2013).

58. Peter Reuell, "When Bias Hurts Profits," *Harvard Gazette*, February 22, 2017, http://news.harvard.edu/gazette/story /2017/02/when-bias-hurts-profits/.

59. Sylvia Ann Hewlett, with Kerrie Peraino, Laura Sherbin, and Karen Sumberg, *The Sponsor Effect: Breaking through the Last Glass Ceiling* (Cambridge: Harvard Business Review, 2010).

60. Sylvia Ann Hewlett, Maggie Jackson, and Ellis Cose, with Courtney Emerson, *Vaulting the Color Bar: How Sponsorship Levers Multicultural Professionals into Leadership* (New York: Center for Talent Innovation, 2012).

61. Hewlett et al., *Glass Ceiling* (see note 59).

62. Sylvia Ann Hewlett, Melinda Marshall, and Laura Sherbin, with Barbara Adachi, *Sponsor Effect 2.0: Road Maps for Sponsors and Protégés* (New York: Center for Talent Innovation, 2012), 69.

63. Hewlett et al., *Vaulting the Color Bar* (see note 57), 62.

64. Hewlett et al., *Sponsor Effect 2.0* (see note 62), 76.

65. Unpublished data from Hewlett Consulting Partners Sponsorship engagement, 2014.

66. Unpublished data from Hewlett Consulting Partners Sponsorship engagement, 2014.

67. Hewlett et al., *Sponsor Effect 2.0* (see note 62), 31.

METHODOLOGY

The research consists of a survey, in-person focus groups, and Insights In-Depth® sessions (a proprietary web-based tool used to conduct voice-facilitated virtual focus groups) involving more than 250 people from our Task Force organizations, as well as one-on-one interviews with fifty-six men and women in the US.

The national survey was conducted online or over the phone in October and November 2016 among 3,570 respondents (1,605 men and 1,965 women; 374 black, 2,258 white, 393 Asian, 395 Hispanic) between the ages of twenty-one and sixty-five currently employed full-time in white-collar occupations, with at least a bachelor's degree. Data were weighted to be representative of the US population on key demographics (age, sex, education, race/ethnicity, and Census Division). The base used for statistical testing was the effective base.

The survey was conducted by NORC at the University of Chicago under the auspices of the Center for Talent Innovation, a nonprofit research organization. NORC was responsible for the data collection, while the Center for Talent Innovation conducted the analysis.

In the charts, percentages may not always add up to 100 because of computer rounding or the acceptance of multiple responses from respondents.

ACKNOWLEDGMENTS

The authors are deeply grateful the sponsors of this research—AllianceBernstein, Bloomberg LP, Bank of America, BP, Cardinal Health, Deutsche Bank, Ernst & Young LLP, Freddie Mac, GlaxoSmithKline, Interpublic Group, Intuit, Johnson & Johnson, Ogilvy & Mather, Sodexo, and Swiss Re—for their generous support. We would also like to thank the cochairs of the Task Force for Talent Innovation—Cynthia Bowman, Erika Irish Brown, Isabel Cruz, Ray Dempsey, Yrthya Dinzey-Flores, Gail Fierstein, Cassandra Frangos, Trevor Gandy, David Gonzales, Wanda Hope, Rosalind Hudnell, Patricia Langer, Janeen Latini, Kendall O'Brien, Lisa Garcia Quiroz, Craig Robinson, Shari Slate, David Tamburelli, Eileen Taylor, Nancy Testa, Duncan Thomas, Kendra Thomas, Karyn Twaronite, Cheryl Wade, and Anré Williams—for their vision and commitment.

Thanks to the private sector members of the Task Force for Talent Innovation for their practical ideas and collaborative energy: Rachael Akohonae, Jennifer Allyn, Rohini Anand, Jolen Anderson, Diane Ashley, Nadine Augusta, Ken Barrett, Ann Bohara, Birgit Boykin, Wendy Myers Cambor, Fiona Cannon, Christy Caragol, Myrna Chao, Rachel Cheeks-Givan,

Tenley Chepiga, Jyoti Chopra, Janessa Cox, Rhonda Crichlow, Cedric Deal, Nancy Di Dia, Jonathan Beane, Nicole Erb, Barbara Evanchik, Alicia Fabé, Hedieh Fakhriyazdi, Grace Figueredo, Joy Fitzgerald, Kent Gardiner, Heide Gardner, Amber Haggins, Maja Hazell, Terry Hogan, Wema Hoover, Gwen Houston, Celia Pohani Huber, Arlene Isaacs-Lowe, Sarah Johnson, Panagiotis (Pete) Karahalios, Shannon Kelleher, Laurie Kowalevsky, Rosemarie Lanard, Janice Little, Heather Lord, Marilu Marshall, Jonathan McBride, Sylvester Mendoza, Michele Meyer-Shipp, Chris Michel, Carolanne Minashi, Kristen Mleczko, Terilyn Monroe, Meredith Moore, Ruth Moore, Brinda Murty, Tricia Myers, Kathleen Navarro, Elise Neef, Deloria Nelson, Birgit Neu, Elizabeth Nieto, Jennifer O'Lear, Adebola Osakwe, Cindy Pace, Jimmie Paschall, Cara Peck, Donna Pedro, Adrienne Penta, Sara Piccollo, LaTonia Pouncey, Danyale Price, Melanie Priddy, Susan Reid, Brandi Riggins, Lynda Risser, Kassi Rushing, Aida Sabo, Claudia Segers, Mary Sellers, Sapna Shah, Deborah Rosado Shaw, Ellyn Shook, Darlene Slaughter, Maria Stolfi, Karen Sumberg, Sandye Taylor, Victoria Thrasher, Brian Tippens, Ara Tucker, NV "Tiger" Tyagarajan, Anilu Vazquez-Ubarri, Vera Vitels, Lynn O'Connor Vos, Barbara Wankoff, Rainia Washington, Irene Waxman, Jacqueline Welch, James White, Kathleen Wishashan, and Nadia Younes.

Thanks also to Pooja Agarwal, Michelle Almeida, Maribel Arias, Subha Barry, Jenifer Beaudean, Carissa

Begonia, Deirdra Bigley, Janique Broomes, Lena Bjurner, Aubrey Blanche, Yvonne Breitenfeld, Kate Burke, Dianne Campbell, Cathy Christian, Arthur Chip Cotton, Jennifer Correa, David Cuberes, Tiffany Daugherty, Beth Ann Day, Robert Dibble, Andrew Ditty, Stephen Dunmore, Makiko Eda, Lily Eng, Lourdes Fisher, Chris Grail, Nefertiti Greene, Anil Gulati, Drew Gulley, Lisa Gutierrez, Sheila Hooda, Mike Huang, Jane Hyun, Wayne Irons, Melissa James, Neene Jenkins, Daphne Jett, Juan Jimenez , Nat Jones, Mike Kaufmann, Sonelius Kendrick-Smith, Philippe Krakowsky, Seema Kumar, Ron Lee, Jenny Lee, Pete Macakanja, Stephen Maire, Sarita Medina, Birthe Mester, Patrick Mlauzi, Loren Monroe-Trice, Raul Morales, Bob Noonan, Adriana Ocampo, Terri O'Connell, RaeAnne Pae, Kerrie Peraino, Chris Perkins, Marie Rineveld, Greg Rutherford, Chuck Sevola, Fran Sharp, Joel Stevens, Chris Thangaraj, Kimberly Warne, Kathleen Widmer, Johnny Wilson, Rachel Yoon, and the other women and men who took part in interviews, focus groups, and Insights In-Depth® sessions.

ADDITIONAL PUBLICATIONS

KEEPING TALENTED WOMEN ON THE ROAD TO SUCCESS

Ambition in Black and White: The Feminist Narrative Revised
Center for Talent Innovation, June 2016

The Power of the Purse: Engaging Women Decision Makers for Healthy Outcomes
Sponsors: Aetna, Bristol-Myers Squibb, Cardinal Health, Eli Lilly and Company, Johnson & Johnson, Merck & Co., Merck KGaA, MetLife, Pfizer, PwC, Strategy&, Teva, WPP (2015)

Women Want Five Things
Sponsors: American Express, AT&T, Bank of America, Boehringer Ingelheim USA, Merck KGaA, The Moody's Foundation (2014)

Harnessing the Power of the Purse: Female Investors and Global Opportunities for Growth
Sponsors: Credit Suisse, Deutsche Bank, Goldman Sachs, Morgan Stanley, Standard Chartered Bank, UBS (2014)

Executive Presence: The Missing Link between Merit and Success
HarperCollins, June 2014

Forget a Mentor, Find a Sponsor: The New Way to Fast-Track Your Career
Harvard Business Review Press, September 2013

On-Ramps and Up-Ramps India
Sponsors: Citi, Genpact, Sodexo, Standard Chartered Bank, Unilever (2013)

Executive Presence
Sponsors: American Express, Bloomberg LP, Credit Suisse, Ernst & Young, Gap Inc., Goldman Sachs, Interpublic Group, The Moody's Foundation (2012)

Sponsor Effect 2.0: Road Maps for Sponsors and Protégés
Sponsors: American Express, AT&T, Booz Allen Hamilton, Deloitte, Freddie Mac, Genentech, Morgan Stanley (2012)

Sponsor Effect: UK
Sponsor: Lloyds Banking Group (2012)

Off-Ramps and On-Ramps Japan: Keeping Talented Women on the Road to Success
Sponsors: Bank of America, Cisco, Goldman Sachs (2011)

The Relationship You Need to Get Right
Harvard Business Review, October 2011

Sponsor Effect: Breaking Through the Last Glass Ceiling
Sponsors: American Express, Deloitte, Intel, Morgan Stanley (2010)

Off-Ramps and On-Ramps Revisited
Harvard Business Review, June 2010

Off-Ramps and On-Ramps Revisited
Sponsors: Cisco, Ernst & Young, The Moody's Foundation (2010)

Letzte Ausfahrt Babypause
Harvard Business Manager (Germany), May 2010

Off-Ramps and On-Ramps Germany
Sponsors: Boehringer Ingelheim, Deutsche Bank, Siemens AG (2010)

Off-Ramps and On-Ramps: Keeping Talented Women on the Road to Success
Harvard Business Review Press, 2007

Off-Ramps and On-Ramps: Keeping Talented Women on the Road to Success
Harvard Business Review, March 2005

The Hidden Brain Drain: Off-Ramps and On-Ramps in Women's Careers
Sponsors: Ernst & Young, Goldman Sachs, Lehman Brothers (2005)

LEVERAGING MINORITY AND MULTICULTURAL TALENT

Easing Racial Tensions at Work
Sponsors: BP, Crowell & Moring LLP, Ernst & Young LLP, Interpublic Group, Johnson & Johnson, New York Life, PwC (2017)

Latinos at Work: Unleashing the Power of Culture
Sponsors: American Express, Bank of America, BP, Chubb, Freddie Mac, MetLife, Morgan Stanley, Wells Fargo (2016)

Black Women: Ready to Lead
Sponsors: American Express, AT&T, Bank of America, Chubb Group of Insurance Companies, The Depository Trust & Clearing Corporation, Intel, Morgan Stanley, White & Case LLP (2015)

How Diversity Drives Innovation: A Compendium of Best Practices
Sponsors: Bloomberg LP, Bristol-Myers Squibb, Cisco, Deutsche Bank, EY, Siemens AG, Time Warner (2014)

Cracking the Code: Executive Presence and Multicultural Professionals
Sponsors: Bank of America, Chubb Group of Insurance Companies, Deloitte, GE, Intel Corporation, McKesson Corporation (2013)

How Diversity Can Drive Innovation
Harvard Business Review, December 2013

Innovation, Diversity and Market Growth
Sponsors: Bloomberg LP, Bristol-Myers Squibb, Cisco,
Deutsche Bank, EY, Siemens AG, Time Warner (2013)

**Vaulting the Color Bar: How Sponsorship Levers
Multicultural Professionals into Leadership**
Sponsors: American Express, Bank of America, Bristol-Myers
Squibb, Deloitte, Intel, Morgan Stanley, NBCUniversal (2012)

**Asians in America: Unleashing the Potential of the
"Model Minority"**
Sponsors: Deloitte, Goldman Sachs, Pfizer, Time Warner (2011)

**Sin Fronteras: Celebrating and Capitalizing on the Strengths
of Latina Executives**
Sponsors: Booz Allen Hamilton, Cisco, Credit Suisse, General
Electric, Goldman Sachs, Johnson & Johnson, Time Warner (2007)

Global Multicultural Executives and the Talent Pipeline
Sponsors: Citigroup, General Electric, PepsiCo, Time Warner,
Unilever (2008)

**Leadership in Your Midst: Tapping the Hidden Strengths of
Minority Executives**
Harvard Business Review, November 2005

**Invisible Lives: Celebrating and Leveraging Diversity in the
Executive Suite**
Sponsors: General Electric, Time Warner, Unilever (2005)

REALIZING THE FULL POTENTIAL OF LGBT TALENT

Out in the World: Securing LGBT Rights in the Global Marketplace
Sponsors: American Express, Bank of America, Barclays, Bloomberg LP, BNY Mellon, BP, Chubb Group of Insurance Companies, Deutsche Bank, Eli Lilly and Company, Ernst & Young LLP, and Out Leadership (2016)

The Power of "Out" 2.0: LGBT in the Workplace
Sponsors: Deloitte, Out on the Street, Time Warner (2013)

For LGBT Workers, Being "Out" Brings Advantages
Harvard Business Review, July/August 2011

The Power of "Out": LGBT in the Workplace
Sponsors: American Express, Boehringer Ingelheim USA, Cisco, Credit Suisse, Deloitte, Google (2011)

RETAINING AND SUSTAINING TOP TALENT

Disrupt Bias, Drive Value
Sponsors: AllianceBernstein, Bank of America, Bloomberg LP, BP, Cardinal Health, Deutsche Bank, Ernst & Young LLP, Freddie Mac, GlaxoSmithKline, Interpublic Group, Intuit, Johnson & Johnson, Ogilvy & Mather, Sodexo, Swiss Re (2017)

Mission Critical: Unlocking the Value of Vets in the Workforce
Sponsors: Booz Allen Hamilton, Boehringer Ingelheim USA, Fordham University, Intercontinental Exchange/NYSE, Prudential Financial, The Moody's Foundation, Wounded Warrior Project (2015)

Top Talent: Keeping Performance Up When Business Is Down
Harvard Business Press, 2009

Sustaining High Performance in Difficult Times
Sponsor: The Moody's Foundation (2008)

Seduction and Risk: The Emergence of Extreme Jobs
Sponsors: American Express, BP plc, ProLogis, UBS (2007)

Extreme Jobs: The Dangerous Allure of the 70-Hour Workweek
Harvard Business Review, December 2006

TAPPING INTO THE STRENGTHS OF GEN Y, GEN X, AND BOOMERS

Misunderstood Millennial Talent: The Other Ninety-One Percent
Sponsors: American Express, Baxalta, Ernst & Young LLP, The Moody's Foundation, Novo Nordisk, S&P Global (2016)

The X Factor: Tapping into the Strengths of the 33- to 46-Year-Old Generation
Sponsors: American Express, Boehringer Ingelheim USA, Cisco, Credit Suisse, Google (2011)

How Gen Y & Boomers Will Reshape Your Agenda
Harvard Business Review, July/August 2009

Bookend Generations: Leveraging Talent and Finding Common Ground
Sponsors: Booz Allen Hamilton, Ernst & Young, Lehman Brothers, Time Warner, UBS (2009)

BECOMING A TALENT MAGNET IN EMERGING MARKETS

Growing Global Executives: The New Competencies
Sponsors: American Express, Bloomberg LP, Cisco Systems, EY, Genpact, Goldman Sachs, Intel, Pearson, Sodexo, The Moody's Foundation (2015)

The Battle for Female Talent in Brazil
Sponsors: Bloomberg LP, Booz & Company, Intel, Pfizer,
Siemens AG (2011)

Winning the War for Talent in Emerging Markets
Harvard Business Press, August 2011

The Battle for Female Talent in China
Sponsors: Bloomberg LP, Booz & Company, Intel, Pfizer,
Siemens AG (2010)

The Battle for Female Talent in India
Sponsors: Bloomberg LP, Booz & Company, Intel, Pfizer,
Siemens AG (2010)

The Battle for Female Talent in Emerging Markets
Harvard Business Review, May 2010

PREVENTING THE EXODUS OF WOMEN IN SET

*Athena Factor 2.0: Accelerating Female Talent in Science,
Engineering & Technology*
Sponsors: American Express, Boehringer Ingelheim USA,
BP, Genentech, McKesson Corporation, Merck Serono,
Schlumberger, Siemens AG (2014)

*The Under-Leveraged Talent Pool: Women Technologists on
Wall Street*
Sponsors: Bank of America, Credit Suisse, Goldman Sachs,
Intel, Merrill Lynch, NYSE Euronext (2008)

Stopping the Exodus of Women in Science
Harvard Business Review, June 2008

*The Athena Factor: Reversing the Brain Drain in Science,
Engineering, and Technology*
Sponsors: Alcoa, Cisco, Johnson & Johnson, Microsoft, Pfizer
(2008)

INDEX OF EXHIBITS

INDEX

F

Flex 44
flex workers 15, 25, 86–87, 94–95, 102–103
flight risk 48–49, 56, 69, 70, 74

G

Gallup 72
Gardner, Heide 124
Google 77–78
Greenwald, Anthony 4
Gulley, Drew 116–117
Gutierrez, Lisa 126–127

H

Harvard 91, 96
heat maps 31, 37, 42, 48, 54, 61, 64, 86–87, 94–95, 102–103
Hill, Linda 91
Hope, Wanda Bryant 118, 123
Huang, Mike 41, 44
Hyun, Jane 44

I

IAT. *See* implicit association test
IDEAL 123–125
implicit association test 4–5, 10–11
inclusive leaders 83–84, 91–99, 100, 111–112, 117–118
inherent diversity 4, 85–91
Innovation, Diversity, and Market Growth 3, 73, 91
Insights In-Depth® 111, 137
Intel 105
Interpublic Group Mediabrands 14, 69, 123–125
IPG *See* Interpublic Group Mediabrands

J

Johnson & Johnson 10, 88–90, 117–118, 122–123

W

TASK FORCE FOR TALENT INNOVATION

QBE North America

RBC Capital Markets

S&P Global

Sanofi

Sodexo

Swiss Reinsurance Co.

Thomson Reuters

UBS**

United Way Worldwide

Vanguard

Visa

Weil, Gotshal & Manges LLP

Wells Fargo and Company

White & Case LLP

Willis Towers Watson

WPP

* Merck KGaA (Darmstadt, Germany)

** Steering Committee

As of July 25, 2017

ABOUT THE AUTHORS

Sylvia Ann Hewlett is an economist and the founder and chief executive officer of the Center for Talent Innovation, where she chairs a private sector task force of eighty-six global companies focused on fully realizing the new streams of talent in the global marketplace. She also codirects the Women's Leadership Program at the Columbia Business School. She is the author of fourteen *Harvard Business Review* articles, twelve critically acclaimed nonfiction books including *Winning the War for Talent in Emerging Markets; Forget a Mentor, Find a Sponsor* (named one of the best business books of 2013); and *Executive Presence* (an Amazon "Best Book of the Month" in June 2014). In 2014 she was recognized as the Most Influential International Thinker by HR Magazine and honored by the European Diversity Awards with its Global Diversity Award. Hewlett, who has taught at Columbia and Princeton Universities, earned her BA at Cambridge University and her PhD in economics at London University.

Ripa Rashid is co-president at the Center for Talent Innovation and a managing partner at Hewlett Consulting Partners, specializing in global talent and leadership strategies. She spent over a decade as a management consultant with global firms including Booz & Company, PwC, and Mitchell Madison Group, and held senior positions at MetLife and Time Warner. Rashid is coauthor of *Winning the War for Talent in Emerging Markets: Why Women are the Solution* (Harvard Business Review Press, 2011), *Asians in America: Unleashing the Potential of the "Model Minority,"* the book, *Growing Global Executives: The New Competencies* (Center for Talent Innovation, 2015), as well as numerous reports and whitepapers. Rashid has lived and worked in North America, Europe, Asia, and South America, and speaks four languages. She earned an AB cum laude in astronomy and astrophysics from Harvard University, an MA in anthropology from New York University, and an MBA from INSEAD.

Laura Sherbin is co-president at the Center for Talent Innovation and a managing partner at Hewlett Consulting Partners. She is an economist who specializes in the creation of competitive advantage through inclusion and diversity. She taught "Women and Globalization" at the School of International and Public Affairs at Columbia University, and is a coauthor of *Harvard Business Review* articles "How Diversity Can Drive Innovation," "How Gen Y and Boomers Will Reshape Your Agenda," "Off-Ramps and On-Ramps Revisited," and *Harvard Business Manager* article "Letzte Ausfahrt Babypause" as well as the Harvard

Business Review Research Reports *The Athena Factor: Reversing the Brain Drain in Science, Engineering, and Technology* and *The Sponsor Effect: Breaking Through the Last Glass Ceiling* and CTI reports including *Executive Presence*, among many others. She earned her PhD in economics from American University.